Viva fastrack

BUSINESS STUDIES

Morris Wood
MBA (Audit) ACA

Viva Books Private Limited
New Delhi • Mumbai • Chennai • Kolkata • Bangalore • Hyderabad

First Indian Edition 2007

VIVA BOOKS PRIVATE LIMITED

- 4737/23 Ansari Road, Daryaganj, New Delhi 110 002
  E-mail: vivadelhi@vivagroupindia.net, Tel. 42242200
- Plot No. 76, Service Industries, Shirvane, Sector 1, Nerul, Navi Mumbai 400 706
  E-mail: vivamumbai@vivagroupindia.net, Tel. 27721273, 27721274
- Jamals Fazal Chambers, 26 Greams Road, Chennai 600 006
  E-mail: vivachennai@vivagroupindia.net, Tel. 28290304, 28294241
- B-103, Jindal Towers, 21/1A/3 Darga Road, Kolkata 700 017
  E-mail: vivakolkata@vivagroupindia.net, Tel. 22836381, 22816713
- 7, Sovereign Park Apartments, 56-58, K. R. Road, Basavanagudi, Bangalore 560 004
  E-mail: vivabangalore@vivagroupindia.net, Tel. 26607409, 26607410
- 101-102 Mughal Marc Apartments, 3-4-637 to 641, Narayanguda, Hyderabad 500 029
  E-mail: vivahyderabad@vivagroupindia.net, Tel. 27564481, 27564482

Published by arrangement with

Pascal Educational Services
655 Parramatta Road
Leichhardt, NSW 2040
Australia

ISBN 81-7649-626-X

Published by Vinod Vasishtha for Viva Books Private Limited, 4737/23, Ansari Road, New Delhi 110 002. Printed and bound at Anand Sons, Delhi.

Contents

Foreword	4
Preferred Australian usage of common business terms	5
Formats of financial statements	6
Important financial ratios	9
Preparing a business plan	15
Sources and types of finance	17
Participants in Australian financial markets	19
Alphabetical listing of terms	21

Foreword

Success will come by learning new things fast.
NOT by learning old things better.

J.M. Wood, 1986

This Business Studies Pocket Book has been written to assist students of business in Years 11 and 12 and also those who may be seeking a career in a business organisation or environment. The intention of these definitions and explanations is to enable those with a real interest in their careers to advance their ambitions at a faster rate than others and thereby reach their personal goals more quickly.

Getting a head start in the working world has never been more important. Globalisation is bringing the whole world much closer together through communications, technology, trade, cultures, finance, information, medicine, music, the arts and more. Integration is key to this process.

I wish to thank Suzanne Collings and Michael Lembach for their valuable input into this book.

This book is dedicated to Ms Virginia Frost who has contributed so much in many years of service to school business education.

I believe that an emphasis on seeking better and more efficient methods of doing things, simplicity, innovation, leadership and a positive attitude to every task will always result in:

- career advancement
- work satisfaction
- a rewarding lifestyle
- the greater ability to pass on knowledge.

Challenge your opportunities, and best wishes.

J. Morris Wood
jmwood@enternet.com.au

Preferred Australian usage of common business terms

The following list indicates the preferred Australian usage of common business terms in preference to older usage which may have been used in texts and other less current educational material. The changes in financial statement usage were specified in the Accounting Standards of the Australian Accounting Standards Board (AASB) and the Public Sector Accounting Standards Board (PSASB), taking effect from 1 July 2000.

Preferred term	Older term
abnormal profits/losses	extraordinary profits/losses
Annual Report	Company Report
breakeven	break-even point
budgets	forecasts, projections
business culture	corporate culture
chattel mortgage	hire-purchase, time payment
Chief Executive Officer (CEO)	General Manager
Constitution	Memorandum and Articles of Association
core business	prime function
economic cycle	business cycle, trade cycle
Employment Relations (ER)	Human Resources, Industrial Relations
financial ratios	accounting ratios, ratio analysis
gearing	leverage, debt to equity
income	revenues, rent/interest received
inventories	stocks
Information Technology (IT)	systems
net	Internet, World Wide Web, web
non-current assets	fixed assets

non-current liabilities	long-term liabilities
owners' equity	shareholders' funds, shareholders' equity
payables	accounts payable, trade creditors, creditors
position description	job description
prevention controls	feedforward controls
property	real estate, land and buildings
receivables	accounts receivable, trade debtors, debtors
Statement of Cash Flows	Cashflow Statement
Statement of Financial Position	Balance Sheet
Statement of Financial Performance	Profit & Loss Account, Revenue Statement, Profit Statement
overdraft	bank overdraft, line of credit
venture capital	seed capital

Formats of financial statements

The degree of detail in a financial statement is dependent on whether the business is a public company or not. For example, a public company must consolidate its controlled entities. The following formats are usual for businesses which are not public companies.

Statement of Financial Performance

Previously known as either the Revenue Statement or Profit & Loss Account.

Businessforce 2000 Pty Limited
Statement of Financial Performance
(Previously known as the Revenue Statement)
For the year ended 30 June 2001

2000 $		Note	2001 $	%
	Sales revenues		600 000	
	Other revenues			
	Rents received		15 000	
	Interest received		25 000	
	Profit on sale of assets		10 000	
600 000	***Total operating revenues***		650 000	100.0
	Less:			
400 000	Cost of goods sold (COGS)	1	420 000	64.6
	Opening inventory			
	+ Purchases, freight			
	– Closing inventory			
200 000	**Gross profit**		230 000	35.4
	Less:			
	Operating expenses			
	Administration	2		
	Financial	3		
	Marketing	4		
	Staff	5		
182 000	*Total operating expenses*	6	215 000	33.1
18 000	**Net profit before tax**	7	**15 000**	**2.3**

Notes:

1 COGS comprises Opening inventory + Purchases/freight – Closing inventory.
2 Administration costs eg. phones, printing, computer costs, travel, couriers, etc.
3 Financial costs eg. bank fees, interest, lease costs, etc.
4 Marketing costs eg. advertising, promotions, commissions, distribution costs.
5 Staff costs eg. wages/salaries, superannuation, training, fringe benefits tax, etc.
6 Expense ratios ideally should be shown by category for the past year as well.
7 The tax payable would be calculated when completing the annual tax return after allowing for any tax paid by PAYG through the year.

Statement of Financial Position

There are two types of presentation for the Statement of Financial Position (previously referred to as the Balance Sheet). These examples are for small to large companies, not public companies.

Format 1

Businessforce 2000 Pty Limited
Statement of Financial Position
(Previously known as the Balance Sheet)
As at 30 June 2001

Assets	**$**	**Liabilities**	**$**
Current assets		Current liabilities	
Cash	15 000	Payables	80 000
Receivables	95 000	Overdraft	30 000
Inventories	52 000	Provision for tax	20 000
Short-term deposits	25 000		
Total current assets	***187 000***	***Total current liabilities***	***130 000***
Non-current assets		***Non-current liabilities***	
Property	250 000	Mortgage property	122 000
Plant & equipment	52 000	Hire-purchase	52 000
Furniture & fittings	50 000		
Total non-current assets	*352 000*	*Total non-current liabilities*	*174 000*
		Total liabilities	***304 000***
Intangible assets		**Owners' equity**	
Goodwill		Paid share capital	150 000
Trademarks		Retained profits	55 000
Patents		Reserves	30 000
		Total owners' equity	235 000
Total assets	**539 000**	**Total liabilities & equity**	**539 000**

Notes:

1. The proportions of hire-purchase and mortgage loans repayable within 12 months are considered to be current liabilities. Those amounts due after 12 months are therefore non-current liabilities.
2. Reserves often reflect the revaluation of a property from its historical cost.
3. Intangible assets may have values and may be written off at the discretion of directors when such values may not be present.
4. Short-term deposits or investments are usually capable of withdrawal as required.
5. Inventories are usually valued at the lower amount of cost or net realisable value.
6. Retained profits include past accumulated profits plus the current year as shown in the Statement of Financial Performance.
7. Dividends in public companies are paid from retained profits.
8. A long-term investment, eg. over 12 months, would be included as a non-current asset, eg. investment in specialist medical equipment.
9. For purposes of analysis, comparative figures for the last year are shown.
10. This Format 1 is gradually being superceded by Format 2, as shown next.

Format 2 (Narrative)

Businessforce 2000 Pty Limited
Statement of Financial Position
(Previously known as the Balance Sheet)
As at 30 June 2001

Last Year $		This Year $
	Current assets	
20 000	Cash	15 000
100 000	Receivables	95 000
57 000	Inventories	52 000
75 000	Short-term deposits	25 000
252 000	***Total current assets***	***187 000***
	Non-current assets	
175 000	Property	250 000
0	Plant & equipment	52 000
50 000	Furniture & fittings	50 000
225 000	***Total non-current assets***	***352 000***
	Intangible assets	
0	Goodwill	0
0	Trademarks	0
0	Patents	0
477 000	*Total assets*	539 000
	Less *current liabilities*	
100 000	Payables	80 000
27 000	Overdraft	30 000
00 000	Provision for tax	20 000
127 000	*Total current liabilities*	130 000
	Non-current liabilities	
130 000	Mortgage property	122 000
00 000	Hire-purchase	52 000
130 000	*Total non-current liabilities*	174 000
257 000	*Total liabilities*	304 000
220 000	**Net assets (worth)**	**235 000**
	Owners' equity (shareholders' funds)	
150 000	Paid share capital	150 000
40 000	Retained profits	55 000
30 000	Reserves	30 000
220 000	**Total owners' equity**	**235 000**

Notes:

Refer to the notes under Format 1 which also apply.

Statement of Cash Flows

This sample statement is a guide for small to large companies. The small business often finds this unnecessary due to the closeness of management to its operations. Small business, however, must be in touch with its cash position continually to avoid future financial embarrassment.

Businessforce 2000 Pty Limited
Statement of Cash Flows
For the year ended 30 June 2001

Last Year		*This Year*
$	*Cash receipts (flows inwards)*	$
800 000	Cash receipts from sales/receivables	700 000
20 000	Interest and rents received	25 000
20 000	Proceeds from borrowings	42 000
840 000	*Total cash receipts*	767 000
	Cash payments (flows outwards)	
(782 000)	Payments for inventories, expenses	(679 000)
(175 000)	Payments for property, plant	(127 000)
(10 000)	Repayment of borrowings	(8 000)
(30 000)	Interest and other finance costs paid	(28 000)
(6 000)	Income tax paid	(5 000)
(1 003 000)	*Total cash payments*	(847 000)
(163 000)	*Net increase (decrease) in cash held*	(80 000)
258 000	*Cash at beginning of financial year*	95 000
95 000	*Cash at the end of the financial year*	15 000

Facilities available to business

Interest bearing deposit at NAB	25 000
Bank overdraft – balance available	85 000
Total facilities available	110 000

Notes:

1 Continual supervision is required of cash availability.

2 A helpful statement to management might include an analysis of receivables overdue and inventory levels since the last period.

3 This form of statement, while helpful, is more likely to be used by larger small businesses. Public companies must report under the headings Operations, Investing and Financing Activities.

Important financial ratios

Ratios in this section will be classed into two major categories: those that are vital for exam purposes (the primary ratios) and those that are used in the public arena (the secondary ratios).

Primary ratios

It is very important to know what these ratios really tell us in terms of a business's status. Thus each ratio listed here will fit into one of four categories: liquidity (solvency), profitability, stability and efficiency

Liquidity (short-term stability/solvency) ratios

1 Current (working capital) ratio
Use: To determine assets available to pay debts.
Benchmark: Better than 1.5 : 1.0
Problems: When assets are less than liabilities.

$$\frac{\textit{Current assets CA}}{\textit{Current liabilities CL}}$$

2 Liquid (quick/acid test) ratio
Use: To determine ability to meet emergencies.
Benchmark: Better than 1.0 : 1.0
Problems: Less than 1.0 : 1.0 may mean a cash crisis pending. May be insolvent. Businesses like Woolworths with high cash flows can operate with lower ratios.

$$\frac{\textit{CA less inventories}}{\textit{CL less overdraft}}$$

Profitability ratios

1 Gross profit ratio
Use: To determine an adequate margin in price.
Benchmark: Depends on industry eg. jewellers 60%; fruiterers 3%. Normal is over 15%.
Problems: Dictated by competition and cost levels.

$$\frac{\textit{Gross profit}}{\textit{Total sales}} \times \frac{100}{1}$$

2 Net profit ratio
Use: To decide drawings, dividends, retained earnings/profits.
Benchmark: Return greater than the inflation rate.
Problems: Must allow sufficient net profit for growth. If too low, mark-up needs review, cost control needs improvement, materials should be sourced more cheaply.

$$\frac{\textit{Net profit after tax}}{\textit{Total sales}} \times \frac{100}{1}$$

3 Return on equity (shareholders' funds)
Use: To determine if owners receive an adequate return (which should be greater than the inflation rate).

$$\frac{\textit{Net profit after tax}}{\textit{Owners' equity}} \times \frac{100}{1}$$

Benchmark: Return greater than the inflation rate.
Problems: If insufficient, could have difficulty raising more capital or funds for working capital.

Stability ratios

1 **Proprietary (or proprietorship) ratio**
Use: To determine the level of owner control.
Benchmark: Desirable over 50%.
Less indicates lenders/creditors may control, eg. 30%

$$\frac{\textit{Owners' equity}}{\textit{Total assets}} \times \frac{100}{1}$$

Problems: Lenders/creditors may have an undesirable influence over the business. Viability may be threatened.

2 **Gearing (leverage/debt to equity) ratio**
Use: To determine the level of borrowings to be serviced from earnings or repaid.

$$\frac{\textit{Total liabilities}}{\textit{Owners' equity}} \times \frac{100}{1}$$

Benchmark: Banks may be up to 80%, public companies to 70%, others less than 50%. High-geared means uses more debt than equity.
Problems: Poor profits will pose problems in servicing debt. Stability may be under threat.

3 **Interest cover ratio**
Use: To determine the number of times interest payments are covered. Based on earnings before interest and tax (EBIT).

$$\frac{\textit{EBIT}}{\textit{Interest expense}}$$

Benchmark: Bankers would be concerned if less than three times.
Problems: Further borrowing harder. Profits would need to be higher. Firms should consider factoring or sale and lease back to lower debt.

Efficiency ratios

1 **Inventory turnover (expressed as number of times p.a.)**
Use: To measure the stock turn rate compared to industry standards and whether levels of stock are too high.

$$\frac{\textit{Cost of goods sold}}{\textit{Opening + closing stock/2}}$$

Benchmark: Depends on the industry. Jewellers may be happy with 2 times p.a, while a fruiterer may be concerned if less than 350 times p.a

2 **Receivables (debtors) turnover (expressed as times p.a. or number of trading days where 365/times)**
Use: To determine the efficiency of the receivables credit and collection policy.

$$\frac{\textit{Total sales (credit)}}{\textit{Opening + closing stock/2}}$$

Benchmark: No greater than 60 days or two months.

Problems: Highlights poor collection effort, doubtful customers/poor payers, inadequate credit checks, poor control over overdues. Bad debts can arise and business viability threatened.

Example: $\frac{\$1\ 200\ 000}{200\ 000}$

6 times p.a. or 365 days/ 6 times = 60.8 *days.*

3 **Expense ratio**

Use: To determine the percentage of each expense to total sales and compare with budgets and the previous year's expenses.

Benchmarks: Will depend on the industry. Budgets will set the standard expense.

Problems: Variances over and under budget will require investigation. Trends over previous years will need analysis.

$$\frac{\textit{Expense item}}{\textit{Total sales}} \times \frac{100}{1}$$

Expressed as a % for each expense and for each category, eg. administration, finance, marketing and staff costs.

Secondary ratios

These ratios are important for investors, public companies, large private companies, creditors and lenders.

Profitability/stability ratios

1 **Dividend per share**

Use: To enable a comparison with other investments. Expressed as a percentage.

$$\frac{\textit{Amount of dividend}}{\textit{Number of ordinary shares issued}}$$

Benchmark: Should be at least equal to inflation rate or better than a short-term investment.

Note: Dividends may be franked, meaning they may already have tax or a portion of the tax paid by the company. Dividends are then not taxed to investors to the extent of the tax paid. If no tax was paid by the company then the dividends are unfranked and therefore taxable to the investors.

2 **Earnings per share (EPS)**

Use: Ideally should show an increase on previous years. Shown in Annual Reports. Continuously monitored by investors.

$$\frac{\textit{Net profit after tax – abnormals}}{\textit{Number of ordinary shares issued}}$$

Note: EPS can vary depending on the type of business. High technology companies tend to spend much on development and hence EPS may temporarily lessen.

3 **Dividend yield**

Use: An indicator of risk. The higher the risk, the greater the yield but if the price is depressed this must also be taken into account. Is a measure of stability when a dividend is paid and increasing.

$$\frac{\textit{Dividend per share}}{\textit{Current share price ASX}}$$

4 **Earnings yield**

Use: To determine the return compared to other investments.

$$\frac{\textit{Earnings per share (EPS)}}{\textit{Current share price ASX}}$$

5 **Price earnings (PE) ratio**

Benchmark: A good company may range from 15 to 30.

Note: The new technology 'revolution' and love affair with the Internet has seen PEs over 400. The risk in the price is then seen as speculative.

$$\frac{\textit{Current share price ASX}}{\textit{Earnings per share (EPS)}}$$

6 **Net assets backing per share**

Benchmark: Should be at least worth more than par value or issue price.

$$\frac{\textit{Total assets} - \textit{liabilities}}{\textit{Number of issued ordinary shares}}$$

Note: Some companies may have very high values and would be seen as attractive by others. Care should be taken as some asset values in the Statement of Financial Position, e.g. property may be in at historical cost and not current valuation.

Comparative analysis

Analysis through ratios may be used to:

- compare one year with others
- compare one company with others in the same industry from interfirm data (such as Dun & Bradstreet) where standard data per industry is available
- compare planned ratios with actual results
- establish benchmarks for a business.

It can also indicate:

- the strengths and weaknesses of a firm
- how the business compares with others
- what the risks are
- the earning potential of the business.

Preparing a business plan

A business without a plan will:

- find difficulty obtaining finance
- lack credibility with suppliers
- not perform to the expectations of owners
- fail within five years, according to past trends.

1	Executive summary	An overview of the plan, ideally on two pages showing the business name and commencement date, product base, target markets, business objectives showing expected sales, profits, and major strategy to get there.
2	Historical background	Owners, start date, product range and results.
3	Situational analysis (including a SWOT analysis)	Identifies present position of the business, its growth, markets, competitors, results to date, organisation structure, employee base and skills, suppliers, internal and external influences on the business and any sustainable competitive advantage.
4	Vision/mission statement	The core purpose written for one year (Mission) in a clear statement of not more than ten words. Use of a Vision statement to say 5 years is optional.
5	Objectives	Production outputs, sales target market and share %, net profit in $ and % of sales, geographic expansion, new products, research, etc.
6	Strategic/operational and production/ marketing plans	Supplier contracts, production scheduling, outputs, plant maintenance, quality targets and inventory levels for production plans. Marketing plans will include products to target markets, pricing mark-ups, promotion strategies, distribution methods, customer servicing. The four P's (product, price, promotion and place) need to be addressed here.
7	Financial budgets	Forecast sales, costs of goods sold, expenses, net profit and cash flows. Also capital expenditure forecast. Cost-benefit or breakeven analysis. Forecast ratios (optional).
8	Finance requirements	Finance needs, eg. overdraft, term loans, etc.
9	Staff budgets	Staff numbers, needs and costings with the total incorporated into staff expenses in the financial budgets.
10	Implementation	Timetable for performance.
11	Review and responsibility	Review timetable for results at least quarterly (usually monthly).

The planning cycle

- Normally commences before the end of the previous financial year and stems from wider Board perspectives.
- The management team, ideally including employee representatives, review initial situational/SWOT analyses by Financial Controllers (public companies).
- Mission/objectives for the year are decided.
- Production/Marketing divisions prepare their respective plans.
- Financial budgets, finance requirements and staff needs prepared and reviewed by management team.
- Accepted budgets and operational plans presented to the Board for approval or amendment before 30 June.
- All staff incorporated into budget expectations for the new financial year. Managers may prepare action plans for individual staff for later performance measurement and appraisal.

Notes

- The degree of detail of the business plan depends on the size and complexity of the business.
- The mission statement is usually short-term and covers 1–2 years, while a long-term strategy may involve a vision statement for up to 3–5 years.
- Actual performance against budget is reviewed monthly as well as inventory levels and receivables overdue.
- Management must always address change to remain competitive and apply teamwork to problem-solving.

Sources and types of finance

This information is included to demonstrate the difference between *sources* of finance and *types* of finance. The *source* is where finance may be obtained, while the *type* of finance refers to the form of borrowing which is used.

Sources of finance	**Types of finance**
Commercial banks	Bank overdrafts, term loans, mortgages over property, commercial bills, debenture loans over assets of a company, personal loans, bridging finance, letters of credit, leasing, factoring (not all banks include in service range), inventory loans, hire-purchase, forward cover and hedging facilities, bank guarantees, trade finance (exports and imports).
Finance companies Note: Risk levels are higher than banks. Rates are therefore marginally higher.	Personal loans, mortgages, hire-purchase, bridging finance, debenture loans over company assets, dealer/inventory financing, finance leasing, term loans, receivables (invoice discounting), inventory financing, property development loans, term loans, trade finance.
Investment banks Note: Mainly service larger or listed businesses.	Investment/term loans, underwriting guarantees, derivatives trading, mortgages, bridging loans, property development loans, intercompany loans, trade finance, debenture loans over company assets.
Building Societies Credit Unions Insurance companies Superannuation funds Solicitors/accountants	Personal loans, hire-purchase, property mortgages, property development finance (strict criteria), term loans, debenture loans over company assets.
Specialist lease companies and equipment suppliers	Finance leasing, operating leasing, leveraged equity leasing, hire-purchase, inventory/dealer financing.
Factoring companies	Factoring, invoice discounting, trade finance, international factoring.
Listed public companies	Intercompany advances usually overnight or short-term to 90 days or thereabouts. Usually unsecured.

Notes

- Finance in a business may come from equity, borrowing (debt), the sale of assets (which in some cases may be leased back), the sale of receivables or inventory (factoring) or from cash generated from retained earnings/profits.
- Borrowings should always be suitable to the purpose for which the funds are required, eg. purchase of a property may require a long-term borrowing, whereas funds for more inventories would use short-term borrowings or overdraft.
- Inventory may be sold to a financier but remain on the seller's premises and on sale to wholesalers or consumers, sales convert to a receivable, eg. vineyard inventories which mature over a long period may be inventoried in this manner.

Participants in Australian financial markets

As well as individuals and businesses, the following entities are the major intermediaries and participants in Australian capital markets.

1 **Reserve Bank of Australia** Acts as banker for the government, implements monetary policy independently but in conjunction with the government of the day; supervises commercial banks and foreign exchange rates; manages coin and note issues; monitors economic data.

2 **Investment banks** Major participants in the short-term money markets; deal with all money market instruments, eg. commercial bills; act as primary advisors to corporations seeking to issue shares or debentures/bonds; underwriters of new share/debenture issues; tender and deal in government securities. Foreign exchange dealers operate in the short-term money market. Many niche market financial services form a part of their activities. They also operate in superannuation funds management, overseas securities and buy/sell in overseas markets. The same can be said of banks.

3 **Commercial banks** Provide customers with a range of products including deposit and cheque accounts, credit/debit cards, personal loans, mortgages, business finance by way of bank bills, debentures, leasing, overdrafts, fixed rate loans, foreign exchange products, ATMs and EFTPOS facilities. Some add other services such as investment services, safe custody, wills, personal advisory and funds management services. Generally hold 'lender of last resort' status from the Reserve Bank. This is usually exercised by influencing other parties to merge or take up a delinquent party's interests rather than allow a bank to fail.

4 **Money market dealers** These dealers buy and sell government securities on the secondary market and offer cash or deposit facilities to major corporations by providing a vital source of liquidity for holders of these assets. They are strictly supervised and monitored by the Reserve Bank and APRA. Many large companies use money market dealers for offloading substantial surplus funds and borrowing short-term for temporary cash shortages.

5 **Finance companies** Are major providers of instalment, business finance, factoring, leasing and property financing. This area is reducing in that the major participants are now AGC (Westpac), ESANDA (ANZ), GE Capital, CBFC (Commonwealth). There are a number of smaller specialist financiers.

6 **Insurance companies** Major participants in the investment of insurance/superannuation funds in domestic and commercial mortgages, property developments, bonds, shares and government securities, and in the derivatives and international portfolio markets. Insurance companies may be the major shareholder in our major trading corporations such as BHP, CRA, etc.

7 **Superannuation funds** Since superannuation contributions by employers were made compulsory, many approved superannuation funds have been established. Many of these funds must invest substantial amounts and at the same time cater for diversity or risk spread and the selected criteria of member contributors. Their impact in capital markets is now enormous.

8 **Building Societies/Credit Unions** Subject to the control and supervision of the Australian Prudential Regulatory Authority (APRA), such organisations make advances to customers for housing and personal loans, and provide a measure of protection to their depositors.

Facilitators

Australian capital markets require the active involvement of two major facilitators, both of which play an educational and supervisory role:

- the Australian Stock Exchange (ASX), and
- the Sydney Futures Exchange (for derivative trading).

A

ABN *See* Australian Business Number.

Introduced with the GST.

ABS *See* Australian Bureau of Statistics

abnormal profits (losses) Profits and losses incurred in the present year which arise from a one-off transaction. *See also* extraordinary profits.

For example, sale of a business division, subsidiary company or investment.

ACCC *See* Australian Competition and Consumer Commission.

accountability The duty to justify your actions in your areas of responsibility: to your superiors, peer group, parents or others to whom you have this obligation.

People have duties and responsibilities, eg. to obey the law, be ethical, complete work tasks properly, etc.

accounting rate of return The net profit from an investment, calculated as a percentage of the cost of the investment.

One method of determining an investment return (ARR).

accounting ratios *See* p. xi.

accounting standards (conventions) Minimum requirements agreed by professional bodies for reporting and administering accounting tasks.

All public businesses must accord. Auditors oversee.

accounts payable Amounts owed by a business to suppliers (trade creditors) for goods and services supplied. Appear as current liabilities in the Statement of Financial Position (Balance Sheet).

Accounts owing for expenses, materials or product purchases bought on credit (usually on 30 days).

accounts receivable Amounts owed to the business by customers who have

Businesses which sell their products or services on

bought goods and services from the business on credit. Appear as current assets in the Statement of Financial Position (Balance Sheet) as Receivables (Debtors).

credit will debit these from Accounts Receivable (Debtors) and credit revenues in the accounting records.

accrual accounting Recording expenses that have been incurred but not yet paid, and recording revenues for sales that have not yet been received in the accounting records of a business.

As distinct from cash accounting, where entries are only recorded when monies are received or when expenses are paid.

acquisition The term used within the GST regime when referring to purchases made by a business which have GST included in their prices.

action plans Specific plans for staff which set out what is to be done, the time frame and the resources to be used. These plans come from overall strategy and operational planning objectives.

A personal timetable for individual staff planning and implementation.

ACTU Australian Council of Trade Unions, the peak national body of most trade unions.

Usually promotes national issues, eg. national wage case.

administration The cost centre in a business which handles the accounting, budgeting, recording, reporting and allied functions. Also a business is said to be 'under administration' when the owners appoint an administrator to trade it out of difficulty or to avoid liquidation.

Other major cost functions of a business may be finance, marketing, research and development, production or operations.

administration expenses (costs) Those costs related to the accounting and related office functions.

Printing, wages, phones, rent, etc.

advertising Using all types of media — newspapers, television, radio, letterbox drops and outdoor signs — to increase product sales or awareness.

Is a marketing expense under the control of a Marketing Manager.

affirmative action Any action in the workplace that will actively hire or promote people that have traditionally been discriminated against in the labour market, eg. women, people with disabilities and minority cultural groups. Employers are required by legislation to implement affirmative action.

Aims to make all employees equal regardless of race, gender, beliefs, culture or age.

agenda A listing of items to be discussed at a meeting on a specified date and time and place.

Includes previous minutes, treasurer's report, etc.

agent An individual or business firm acting on behalf of another (the principal).

A manufacturer will be a principal and a retailer the agent.

All Ordinaries Index (AllOrds) The index of all listed public company shares as determined by the Australian Stock Exchange. Reflects movements in prices.

Struck for publication daily. Other indices include ASX 200, the top 200 listed shares by trading volume.

Annual General Meeting (AGM) The meeting required by the *Corporations Law* to be held each year in a public company. Shareholders of a company receive, discuss and adopt the financial reports of the company and attend to other company matters on which the Board seeks their direction.

Also votes for directors and auditors in a public company. Concerns of shareholders are heard.

Annual Report A yearly report to shareholders comprising the Statements

All public companies must be audited and an

of Financial Performance, Position and Cashflow along with a Directors' Report. Strict standards are required for presentation.

Auditors' Report included. in the Annual Report

annual return A report filed by all companies with ASIC each year. Under review.

Confirms directors, registered office and that a company is still operating.

anti-discrimination Business behaviour that ensures that all people receive the same fair and equal treatment in the workforce regardless of age, gender, cultural background, etc. *See also* affirmative action.

Anti-discrimination legislation is in place to regulate this. Only merit should be the discriminator.

appreciation The increase in the value of an asset or a currency as against other currencies over time.

Property usually appreciates in value over time.

apprenticeship Where an employee with government assistance joins an employer for on-site trade training and also receives instruction at educational schools with the intent of obtaining a formal trade certificate.

Apprenticeships are commonly taken for metal trades, plumbing, electrical, motor mechanic, hairdressing, etc.

APRA *See* Australian Prudential Regulatory Authority.

arbitrage The trading process of taking advantage of differing rates, prices or conditions between different capital markets or security maturities.

Buying in one market and selling the same commodity in another to make a profit.

arbitration The process of settling a dispute before an impartial umpire, court or tribunal.

Use of an independent party where negotiation between the original parties cannot progress.

Articles of Association A document setting out the basic rules of conduct for a company, which with a Memorandum of Association is filed with ASIC when a new company is registered. Now incorporated into the new Constitution (from 2000).

May be adopted from a standard or varied as required. Constitution is the new name for the Articles and Memorandum.

artificial intelligence Computers that have been programmed to make decisions based on certain input data.

The programs that activate computers to respond to certain events.

ASIC *See* Australian Securities and Investment Commission.

assets Items of monetary value owned or controlled by a business. Can be tangible, such as cash, inventories, plant and equipment, motor vehicles and property, or intangible, such as goodwill, patents and trademarks. Shown on the Statement of Financial Position (Balance Sheet).

Assets may be current when expected to be converted to cash within 12 months, or non-current when expected to generate revenue over a period longer than 12 months.

ASX *See* Australian Stock Exchange.

asset-backed security A bond issued in capital markets backed by strong financial assets such as property mortgages, leases, personal loan portfolios, etc. The securitisation of financial assets is a growing industry.

Have strict guidelines for issuance, with trustees appointed, credit insurance and strong credit ratings.

attrition A reduction in a workforce due to the resignation of employees.

Usually through poor management or staff preference.

audit The undertaking of an extensive review of the accounting records, proce-

Usually carried out at least twice a year. Larger firms

dures and presentation of a business by an independent accounting firm.

use an internal audit team for ongoing compliance checking.

auditor An independent accounting firm which must be appointed by public companies to carry out a detailed review of business records, procedures and reporting presentations. An Auditors' Report must be appended to the Annual Report each year.

Other businesses have the option of appointing their own auditors, especially where there are substantial minority interests.

Australian Bureau of Statistics (ABS) A Federal Government agency charged with collecting, analysing and distributing social, economic and business statistics. See website at **www.abs.gov.au**

Data is used by governments and business for management decisions.

Australian Business Number (ABN) The number allocated by the Australian Tax Office when a business registers for GST. Businesses then claim input tax credits and pay the GST collected to the ATO.

If business income is less than $50 000 there is no need to register. A business earning more must register or have 48.5% of each invoice for sales deducted.

Australian Chamber of Commerce and Industry (ACCI) A peak body representing all Chambers of Commerce and their members when dealing with industry and governments. See website at **www.acci.asn.au**

Chambers of Commerce are numerous throughout Australia. Their members comprise local businesses and social groups.

Australian Competition and Consumer Commission (ACCC) A Federal Government statutory authority which monitors all aspects of fair competition under trade practices legislation and market pricing under prices surveillance legislation. See website at **www.accc.gov.au**

Unfair trading, market collusion in pricing and mergers that may reduce reasonable competition are examples of their activity.

Australian Council of Social Services (ACOSS) The peak welfare body covering social and welfare lobby groups in Australia.

See website at **www.acoss.org.au**

Australian Industrial Relations Commission (AIRC) The specialist body with delegated authority from the Industrial Court to resolve disputes of an interstate and industrial nature. See website at **www.dir.gov.au**

Its decisions dominate the industrial relations environment.

Australian Pacific Economic Community (APEC) *See* Pacific rim.

Australian Prudential Regulatory Authority (APRA) A Federal Government statutory enterprise with responsibility for regular supervision of the financial viability of credit unions, building societies, insurance companies and superannuation funds to provide confidence to governments and users.

Enforces strict compliance for nominated institutions. In accountability it ranks after the directors, management and auditors.

Australian Securities and Investment Commission (ASIC) The government body responsible for administering the *Corporations Law* and also supervising business practices and ethics.

Administers business names, company registration, directors' compliance, filing of annual returns, etc.

Australian Stock Exchange (ASX) The national Australian capital market that facilitates the trading of securities and financial instruments. Its members act as intermediaries in the buying and selling of such instruments. See website at **www.asx.com.au**

Also provides education, oversees listing requirements and monitors price movements and company advices.

A

Australian Taxation Office (ATO) The government agency collecting taxes and GST.

See website at **www.ato.gov.au**

autocrat A manager who keeps all the powers of decision-making which employees must accept.

Staff have no say and do as they are told. Does not achieve best results.

authorised capital The maximum amount of capital able to be raised by a company. Shown in the Constitution (previously the Memorandum of Association) when a company is established.

Issued capital may be paid up or partially paid up and is a proportion of the authorised capital.

authority The right to take action, get things done or have the ability delegated from others to do so.

For example, the Employment Relations Manager may have the authority to hire new staff.

award A legally enforceable agreement between unions and employers covering minimum pay and working conditions.

Industry awards are now complemented by enterprise bargaining agreements.

B

bad debt A receivable (account receivable) which cannot be collected. It may be written off as an expense in the Statement of Financial Performance (Revenue Statement or Profit & Loss Account) if legal action has been taken to recover it.

If the debt is recovered later it must be taken in as income where it had previously been written off. Bad debts may reflect poor credit controls.

balance day adjustments Changes made in accounting records at the end of the financial period relating to transactions which have not been completed within the period.

Balance of Payments (BOP) Is the record of a country's trade and financial transactions with the rest of the world. Usually issued quarterly by governments.

An important indicator of the country's economic trends for government to manage.

balance sheet The financial statement of a business that shows the amounts owned and owed by a business at a point in time. Present use is now Statement of Financial Position (Balance Sheet) which is read with the Statement of Financial Performance (Revenue Statement or Profit & Loss Account) showing a business's net profit or loss.

Assets are owned, eg. inventories; liabilities are owed, eg. loans.

Equity = Owners' funds

Assets = Liabilities + Owners' Equity

bank A commercial trading institution and the dominant financial institution in the Australian environment. Trading bank licences have been extended to newer banks with overseas interests since the 1980s.

The term 'bank' in the title is authorised by the Federal Treasurer. Banks are the primary point of contact for all business and personal finance needs.

bank lines Loans made by banks which are either drawn or able to be drawn by businesses.

Term loans, overdrafts and trade accommodation are lines of credit.

bank reconciliation The balancing of the cash shown as held in the business cashbook with the bank statement as at the same date.

There are times when deposits may not be recorded at the bank. Cheques not yet presented to the bank will show as outstanding.

bankruptcy The state of not being able to pay debts. A person is declared bankrupt by the courts.

A bankrupt must sell all assets except personal effects, tools of trade and transport.

bans Refusals by employee or employee groups to carry out their regular work for a specific reason.

Occur over wages, conditions, health and safety or other dispute.

BAS *See* Business Activity Statement.

basis point One hundredth of 1%. Used in capital markets when referring to interest rates and yields.

Used in ASX and SFE and by intermediaries.

batch production The production of a specific order in which all the items produced have the same specification.

Usually a number of the same product. *See also* piece production

bear market A situation in which there is a sustained fall in share or money market prices which do not offer a quick recovery for investors. Characterised by sustained selling.

Bear investors are people who believe prices are going down and interest rates are heading up. Bad news can trigger sales.

behavioural management A theory of management used 1890–1950 that recognised the importance of staff contribution. Signified emerging democracy in the workplace.

Came after the classical/scientific (Taylor) theory of 'do as you are told'.

benchmark A desirable point of reference used to assess actual results.

Measures quality, excellence and performance.

bilateral trade Trade between two countries under specific agreements that give each country some benefit, eg. the Closer Economic Relations (CER) agreement between Australia and NZ.

Recently superseded by countries being brought into trading blocks, eg. the EU, NAFTA, ASEAN.

Bill of Exchange An unconditional order, signed by the person giving it, requiring the person to whom it is addressed to pay a specified amount to a particular person or to the bearer on a specified date. Bills may be trade or accommodation.

A drawer draws the bill; an acceptor accepts it and an endorser (on its reverse) accepts the bill when selling on. Bills are traded in money markets.

biotechnology Technology related to the use of or research into living cells or bacteria in industry.

An emerging area for research with recent DNA cell mapping.

Board of Directors The policy and advisory body representing owners which oversees the operations and management of a company. Meets regularly to review performance and any remedial course of action. Approves new directions for management implementation.

Sets policies and directions, and reviews progress of a business. A Board is elected annually and must adhere to strict corporate regulations.

bond Usually issued by governments in return for cash deposited for a specified period of time, earning interest for the lender. A type of IOU.

After initial issue can be traded in capital markets. A good credit rating is preferred.

bonus shares Free shares issued to existing shareholders in proportion to their shareholdings. Issuing will increase the business's share capital.

A form of return to the investor as well as or instead of dividends. Traded if listed.

bottom line Colloquial term to mean the net profit or loss of a business.

An added cost will affect the 'bottom line'.

brand The name, trademark or symbol for a product or service which distinguishes it from others

breakeven Occurs when the total revenues of a business are equal to its total costs, or where no profit

The formula for breakeven is:

$$\frac{\text{Total fixed costs}}{\text{Sales price} - \text{Variable cost}}$$

or loss is made. Also known as the *break-even point*.

broker An intermediary who handles specific industry tasks between the consumer and the capital or supply markets. For example, an insurance broker seeks out the best insurance policy for a consumer from the range of companies offering insurance products, while a stockbroker handles the buying and selling of securities for a client.

There are also mortgage brokers, marine brokers, finance brokers and so on.

brokerage Commission charged by an intermediary (broker) between buyer and seller.

Investment banks and stockbrokers charge brokerage.

budgets Projections of sales, expenses, profits and staff/capital needs for a selected period. Used as the base for comparing actual results.

A vital management planning tool to measure performance and correct variations.

building societies Financial institutions whose original objectives were to provide housing finance from deposits made in savings accounts.

Deregulation has seen amalgamations and some have become banks, eg. St George.

bull market Situation characterised by sustained and enthusiastic buying due to the perception of rising prices and falling interest rates.

Sharemarket optimism. Often prompted by good economic and/or corporate news.

bureaucrats Officials of government and quasi-government bodies advising government ministers.

A bureaucracy may also refer to a body of managers which may be averse to change.

Business Activity Statement (BAS) A form, introduced with the GST, which registered businesses must file regularly to the ATO. It declares gross sales, other income (supplies) and payments made (acquisitions) plus the GST that has been applied to each and which must be either paid to the ATO or claimed back from the ATO at each agreed return date. Wage tax deductions are also paid. A PAYG instalment must also be paid quarterly with the BAS return. Small businesses have the option to report quarterly or yearly.

The BAS requires GST to be paid to the ATO for 10% of the value of the products and services sold. A claim on the ATO may be made where payments including a GST component are paid and where the GST exceeds the amount charged on sales (supplies).

business concept development The steps taken when progressing a business idea. This may include sample testing of the product or service, market research, checking government regulations, personal assessment regarding commitment to the concept, available cash/assets for initial start-up, a basic business plan, discussion with a banker/accountant, registration of business name, form of entity from which to operate, location of the business and arrangements with suppliers.

A good development program is a major contributing factor to the success of an enterprise. Using professionals as advisors in the start-up phase can cover areas of weakness by a business owner, since business failure mainly arises through poor management, eg. the failure of HIH, Ansett, OneTel.

business cessation The act of an owner closing a business or being forced by creditors to close through administration and then liquidation.

Business Council of Australia (BCA) The national representative peak body of chief

Negotiates in national wage cases and advises governments.

B

executives of large companies. See website at **www.bca.com.au**

business culture The basic philosophy of a business's management. Ideally, it should create a positive attitude among all employees so they work as a cohesive innovative unit. Also known as *corporate culture.*

The soul of a business: its attitudes, teamwork and sense of wellbeing which create a desirable or miserable work environment.

business entity A company, partnership, trust or simply any firm which trades.

All businesses are entities.

business ethics Fair and honest trading in business. Can be self-imposed by a business or led by the expectations of society. Bad conduct is unacceptable.

Refer to video case study *Ethics & Enterprise* available from the NSW Independent Commission against Corruption (ICAC) at **www.icac.nsw.gov.au**

business environment The internal (within the business) and external (from outside the business) influences which will impact on a business.

Business planning will take these into account, along with a situational analysis.

business life cycle The stages in the growth of a business establishment: starting up, incorporation, growth, maturity, post-maturity, crisis, renewal, cessation.

Growth may be domestic or international. Maturity may lead to decline and failure or to renewal. Singer is a well-known example.

business name The name under which a business trades. Owned by the owner of the business. Must be registered for protection unless owner's name used.

Usually registered at ASIC or as a trademark.

business plan A comprehensive strategy outline which forms the basis for all

Essential elements include products, brief

business operations and is usually undertaken annually. When prepared properly it can improve the availability of finance from lenders. Allows a business to track its progress against its plan. In today's competitive environment annual business plans are necessary. *See* p. xv.

history, objectives, situational/SWOT analysis, budgets, strategic and operational plans, etc.

C

calls When a company has issued partly paid shares and then requests either the full balance remaining or another part balance, this is known as a 'call'.

Shareholders are liable for unpaid shares in a call or winding up.

capital The money or asset value introduced into a business by its owner. Forms part of the owners' equity showing in the Statement of Financial Position (Balance Sheet).

Owners' equity includes capital, retained profits and reserves.

capital assets *See* fixed assets.

capital equipment Comprises non-current assets (fixed assets) used in producing products. Also includes support equipment such as motor cars, computers, etc.

Includes plant and equipment, furniture and fittings, motor vehicles and property.

capital expenditure Money spent on capital equipment. Annual business plans will include a capital expenditure budget for new plant and equipment, motor vehicles, property and so on, which will be acquired in the year.

Government budgets also provide for capital expenditure, eg roads.

cash accounting The recording of entries in accounting records only when cash is received or payments are made.

As distinct from accrual accounting where entries are recorded for credit sales or expenses not yet paid.

cash budget Identifies the cash required throughout the financial period and is based on the budgeted sales, production and expenses. The cash budget will come from existing cash and working capital control. Additional funds may be required for both the short-term (overdraft) and long-term (mortgages, debentures, term loans, equity) needs of a business.

See also cashflow forecasts and Formats of Financial Statements on p. vi.

cash control Constant surveillance by a business over its cash at the bank, available facilities that can be called, overdue status of its receivables, inventory levels, purchasing controls and wastage.

A well-managed business will always know its cash forecasts, how much is in the bank and the amount of facilities available.

cash flow The flow of cash in and out of a business, usually through its bank account. The speed of movement reflects the efficiency of a business in selling products, collecting its receivables and moving its inventories, etc. *See also* Statement of Cash Flows.

This is a vital area for daily review, as shortfalls will require bank facilities being available in times of need.

cash flow forecast (budget) Indicates the expectation of a business in receiving cash from sales, receivables, loans, assets sales and from paying costs for materials, expenses, wages, loans, etc. The net of inflows and outflows for the forecast period will indicate to management what

A part of the budgeting process and regularly updated to ensure cash shortfalls are catered for. The cash flow statement will compare the forecast to the actual results.

must be done to increase bank facilities, improve working capital from better collections or quicker inventory movement and so on.

certified agreement An agreement made between employers and employees regarding wages and conditions in a workplace which has been ratified and approved by an appropriate tribunal or commission.

Usually related to one business whereas an award will relate minimum wages and conditions to an entire industry.

certificate of incorporation Issued to a company after registration with ASIC, enabling the business to trade as a legal entity.

For proprietary and public companies, cooperatives, building societies, credit unions and super funds.

chain of command The line of authority from top management through the organisation to the work floor. Accountability extends upwards to each managerial level. *See* organisation structure and induction.

Is evident when an organisation structure of the business has been presented, usually in an induction manual.

change Includes the evolvement of management theories and internal influences from technology, procedures, staff training, organisational structures, and also from external influences such as globalisation, environment groups, the Internet, communications, customers and competition.

The manner in which a business addresses change may determine the success or otherwise of any business. Change is now occurring faster as new technologies are developing.

change charter Included in induction manuals to promote a policy of continual improvement and the benefits expected from such change, such as improved competitiveness, innovation, teamwork,

Now used to good effect in directing employment towards sustainability. Procedures are set out in a change charter to

equity, rewards and continual viability. Progressive businesses are aware that profits employ people hence the importance of a change charter.

facilitate ideas by using quality circles as agents for change.

change model The format required to ensure change is eased into a business culture that will benefit the business and, ideally, employees. This means an induction change charter, internal training at all levels, improved communications, change promotion in quality circles, use of cost/benefit analysis, teamwork, testing, results reviews, extending incentives and implementation.

The change models introduced into Telstra and Westpac are a good guide to adopting change as a policy. See Blount and Joss, *Managing in Australia*, Lansdowne Press, Sydney, 1999.

channels of distribution The differing methods of directing goods or services from the factory/innovator to the customer.

Products may pass from wholesalers to retailers to customers and may include other agents. Disintermediation means cutting out any 'middle people'.

chattel mortgage Where security is taken over specific plant and equipment, motor vehicles, etc, where a loan has been made. *See also* hire-purchase.

Usually defaulting on a loan will see the mortgage called in and the goods recovered by the lender.

Chief Executive Officer (CEO) The senior manager in a business. Known as a Managing Director where he/she is also on the Board of Directors. In smaller businesses may be a General Manager. Responsible for implementing the policies of the Board and directing and supervising senior managers.

As the most senior manager this person is accountable to the Board.

classical/scientific management An early (c. 1850–1920) theory of management based on simple, repetitive work broken down into separate tasks. Characterised by strict standards and autocratic direction.

Was superseded by behavioural management which introduced staff involvement.

closed shop A now almost defunct term to describe a workplace where employees were unable to work unless a member of a particular union.

The closed shop is now illegal as membership of unions in Australia is now voluntary.

code of practice Ethical standards of behaviour in business, often written into manuals. The accepted manner of doing business.

Established by a business, often based on the values of society in general.

coercive power Having the ability to force employees to follow directions under the threat of punishment.

Acceptable in the military forces and in some business situations.

collateral The security given by a business to a lender over assets.

A business may also be said to be collateral to the loan, just as a car is collateral for a loan to buy it.

collective bargaining The negotiation between employers and either employee groups or unions over the terms of an award or enterprise agreement.

Undertaken to agree on wages and conditions prior to new agreements being ratified.

collegial management A style of management where input from the workplace is considered almost equal to that of management.

A management theory often common in small businesses. The *democratic* style is an extension.

commercial bill A bill of exchange, like an IOU, given for a loan for 30–180 days. When a bank is a party or endorses a bill, it may be traded.

A short-term facility offered by banks where the credit is sound.

commodities Products (usually primary industry) which form the basis of Australia's trade. May also be certain products traded in the futures markets.

Wheat, wool, sugar, cotton, gold, silver, etc. Futures markets may trade in pork bellies, soya beans, etc.

common law Law based on the decisions of judges or the common customs of a country rather than Acts of Parliament.

Used where a specific law may not apply.

communication process A management procedure that ensures all participants are adequately and properly informed. Depends on the nature of what is to be communicated but may involve management, employees, the community, industry employer groups, support services and technical advisors (Internet/email servers).

Communication, in both small and large businesses, has traditionally been guarded and of low importance. Now it is vital to business success and continuing viability.

communication methods These depend on the item to be communicated but include memorandum, email, direct advice, advertisements, radio, television, the Internet, sponsorships, product presentation and quality, personal addresses and involvement in community groups.

Communication options are evaluated when product promotions are planned.

company A legal entity separate from the shareholders that set it up. Registered with ASIC. May be a proprietary or public company with limited liability.

Shareholders' liability is limited by their shares or any amount unpaid. A company limited by guarantee may call on shareholders for a set sum on cessation.

comparative ratio analysis Where a business has used ratio analysis to identify levels of profitability, liquidity, efficiency and stability and compared the

Interfirm comparison statistics are maintained by Dun & Bradstreet, a US-based commercial results either with previous years or with companies within the same industry that will give a guide as to performance.

credit agency, and by the University of New England.

competition Where one or more businesses with similar products and services try to get consumers to buy their goods/services in preference to those of other businesses. Competition becomes more intense where the factors of price, quality, service, reputation, costs, structure and distance from the markets can give an advantage.

Competition will be greater with more businesses in the market. ASIC argue that the more competition there is, the better it is for the consumer.

competitive advantage A factor which gives a real advantage over competition.

Microsoft® Windows may be said to have a competitive advantage over Linux, e.g. its extensive use.

compound interest Interest paid on capital plus interest paid on accumulated interest.

The reinvestment of any interest will result in compounding.

Compulsory Third Party (CTP) The type of insurance cover that protects motorists from claims from third parties for damage or injury to their person and some property.

Compulsory throughout Australia when registering motor vehicles.

computer-aided design (CAD) The use of computers and sophisticated graphics to develop new processes, packaging, products, designs, layouts, etc.

An integral part in the progress of manufacturing, new technology and innovation.

conciliation The process by which a dispute is mediated between two or more parties in order to reach a common agreement.

Often employed in union/management disputes involving the Australian Industrial Relations Commission.

concurrent controls Procedures to allow work in production to be properly checked and remedied where necessary. Failure to fix problems will result in higher costs of production, poor quality and faulty outputs.

An example may be staff supervision, checking of materials, error checking, output rates, wastage, etc. *See also* prevention controls & feedback controls.

consensus Process where a group of people agrees on an acceptable decision to all. Does not always result in the best decision as sectional interests can cloud the real intent.

Allows discussion of all viewpoints and options, but some people may be disadvantaged.

consideration That which is received or given in return for a promise or benefit. This is one element of what is needed in a legal contract.

Usually money or some other return benefit.

Constitution In general terms, is a statement of the basic rules of how a country conducts itself. In business, refers to the rules governing a new business, replacing the old Memorandum and Articles of Association.

Australia's constitution requires a majority vote of people and States to effect any change to it. A new business now has a Constitution, e.g. rules for its conduct.

Consumer Price Index (CPI) The measure calculated by the Australian Bureau of Statistics which includes the cost of selected goods or services which represent a basket of products typically affected by price changes. The resulting index is measured against the previous result and for the year to date.

Used by economists as a measure for future economic forecasting and, in turn, for government policy-making.

consumerism The promotion by a group or movement to get better terms and conditions for the buying public.

For example, promotion of some protection for lay-by goods in stores.

contingent liability A liability that may have to be met or paid if certain circumstances occur. Public companies must disclose all or any contingency under accounting standards.

In the Statement of Financial Position the contingent liabilities would be shown as footnotes, eg. operating lease (rental) contracts or potential litigation liabilities.

contingency management A theory of management that sought to allow employees to be directed based on their individual strengths. Flexibility was a key feature and options were available.

Was too 'laissez-faire' as more firm ground rules were needed. It was not found to be positive enough to build teamwork.

contract A written or verbal agreement between two or more parties. Valid if the courts can enforce, but must include certain elements: offer/acceptance, legality, genuine consent, consideration and intent. Bankrupts cannot enter into contracts.

May be void if any of these elements do not exist. A person under 18 years is limited unless for necessities.

contracting out *See* outsourcing.

contract of service A legal arrangement between an employer and employee in which certain conditions will apply. The employer is liable for acts of an employee.

May be evidenced by a letter of appointment or a separate enterprise agreement.

contribution **(1)** A monetary payment. **(2)** The net amount of the selling price less the variable cost of production (known as the *contribution margin*).

Not to be confused with gross profit, which is the selling price less cost of goods sold.

controlling The evaluating, comparing and remedying function within a business. Production/operations control can be preventative, concurrent (for work in progress) or involve feedback. Financial

One of the four management functions in the POLC model (planning, organising, leading, controlling). This sets out

control will compare actual results to budgets and take remedial action if necessary. Management control relates to all areas of the business, often expressed in planning, organising and leading the business towards its objectives.

how management influences overall control in seeking to maximise long-term business results.

convertible notes Debt securities issued on the basis that they may convert to shares at some future time or after a specified event. Able to be traded if in a listed public company. Shares issued may be ordinary or preference.

Initially pay interest to the holder of the security. On conversion to shares the owners would receive dividends or bonus shares.

convertible preference shares Preference shares held by investors in a listed company which pay a fixed rate of return, but where the shares convert to ordinary shares at some future time.

These may also be issued as non-convertible preference shares.

cooperatives Incorporated businesses comprising members with a common interest who obtain mutual benefits. The cooperative is owned and controlled by its members.

Building societies, credit unions and dairy companies are examples.

copyright The exclusive right of a holder to publish, perform, copy or sell an original piece of work. The value of a copyright is shown in a Statement of Financial Position (Balance Sheet) as an intangible asset.

Intangible assets can also include patents, logos, trademarks and goodwill.

core business The main operation or purpose of a business, eg. to produce a product as a manufacturer, sell as a wholesaler/retailer, or provide a service

Usually inherent in the title of a business.

to customers or other businesses. Also known as *prime function.*

corporate culture *See* business culture.

corporate raider A company which seeks to buy shares in another company and then impose its own terms on the business through its increased shareholding. This may result in a new majority owner in the business. Stakeholders must be considered when new majority shareholders obtain control.

Corporate raiders seek to gain cash resources by either selling off assets or acquiring cash resources from the business. This is a legitimate business.

Corporations Law Legislation which determines how companies are set up and how business is conducted, the reporting of financial matters, supervision of ethical practices and procedures towards cessation. Is a combination of relevant Acts.

Administered by the Australian Securities and Investment Commission (ASIC).

cost-benefit analysis The evaluation of all costs and benefits of a project or course of action that enables a comparison with other alternatives.

costing (cost pricing) The assessment of the various costs which make up a component. Costings also include indirect expenses and a profit mark-up.

cost centre An identifiable area within a business which only incurs costs and has no direct revenue. May be a department or area such as production, materials handling, inventory control, warehousing or administration, etc.

Distinct from *profit centres* where revenues would exceed any costs, eg. sales department.

cost of goods sold (COGS) The price paid by a business for the components or goods it later resells. The gross profit of a business arises from the selling price less the cost of goods sold.

Calculated in a Statement of Financial Performance (Revenue Statement or Profit & Loss Account) as
Opening inventory
+ materials purchased
– closing inventory
= cost of goods sold

coupon A voucher attached to certain securities, eg. bonds, which is exchangeable for cash on the due date (usually half-yearly). Represents the annual rate of interest the bond issuer agrees to pay the bondholder.

For example, a 7% coupon will entitle the holder of a bond for $10 000 to half-yearly interest of $350.

creative accounting The presentation of a business's financial position in a misleading manner to present the business as in a stronger position than it actually is.

Also known as 'window dressing'. Accounting standards are intended to stamp it out.

creditor A person or business owed money for the supply or goods or services. *See also* accounts payable.

Shown as a current liability in the Statement of Financial Position (Balance Sheet).

credit policy The terms and conditions a business sets when offering sales on credit. Includes credit applications, checking procedures, terms on invoices and collection controls. A vital management control area to minimise costs and potential bad debts.

Terms may be 30 days, ie. due by end of the next month. Receivable turnover should be no more than 63 days.

credit provider An entity which supplies credit. Various State Credit Acts specify that businesses which provide credit under regulated contracts are licensed.

Regulated contracts are hire-purchase, chattel mortgage, personal loans, etc.

credit ratings Those ratings given by international agencies (Moody's or Standard & Poor's) that evaluate individual securities for their credit, security and ability to repay on time.

The top rating, AAA, indicates a safer security than one with a C rating, for example.

Credit Reference Association (CRA) *See* Data Advantage Ltd (its new name).

credit risk The risk a person would take in entering into a contract or opening an account for another person to pay, or investing in a share or property. This may depend on the credit rating given by a rating agency for a tradable security. Investors may be conservative or speculative, depending on what risk they take.

The higher the perceived risk the greater the interest return, and the greater potential for loss. *See also* risk.

credit union A financial cooperative usually set up within large businesses or industries to service their employees.

Offers personal loans, mortgages, car loans to members and business loans.

credit watch Awaiting a rating or review by a rating agency (eg. Moody's or Standard & Poor's).

When a public company makes a move that may alter its stability it is said to be on 'credit watch'.

critical path analysis The presentation of a sequence of events showing their timings and their relationship to each other. Used in seeking the most efficient method in timing for a project.

Typically used in a building project or equivalent. *See also* PERT.

cumulative preference shares A preference share which pays a set return and which may be accumulated (at the company's discretion) to be

Often issued when a company wants to limit its cash resources and allow a preference to shareholders

paid at a future time, usually for the holder's benefit.

in the event of failure.

currency A country's money. Currency appreciation occurs when the exchange rate of one currency increases in relation to that of another.

If the value of the Australian dollar (AUD) is low, imports will be more costly but export earnings will improve.

currency swap Where two parties exchange an equal amount of two currencies at the spot (today's) exchange rate.

May be initiated by banks or businesses. Part of risk management.

current assets Cash held, inventories, receivables owed to a business and other assets easily converted to cash. Identified on the Statement of Financial Position (Balance Sheet).

As distinct from non-current assets such as property, plant and equipment, furniture and motor vehicles.

current liabilities Amounts owed by a business to external entities, including accounts payable, bank overdrafts and commercial bills. Identified on the Statement of Financial Position (Balance Sheet).

Only amounts owed within 12 months. Amounts owed over 12 months will be non-current liabilities.

current ratio Current assets divided by current liabilities. Ideally should be $2 assets to $1 liabilities, but this will depend on the type of business. A normal business with less than 1:1 would be facing a cash crisis. Also known as the working capital ratio.

Norm is $\frac{CA}{CL}\ \frac{2}{1}$

Fruiterers (high turnover), doctors and dentists will have lower ratios than 1:1.

customer The person or business that benefits from the products or services of others. A *target market* is a group of customers with a certain profile, eg. youth, the elderly.

Customers have certain legislative protection and customer service needs to be good to ensure repeat business.

customer relations Where a business maintains communication with present and past customers, responds to their needs and problems, seeks their advice on products or services, keeps them informed of new products, recalls and provides after-sales service.

It is often said that 'the customer is king' for if customers do not buy again then profits will be affected. Profits employ people.

D

damages An amount payable due to loss or hurt from an improbable event or wrongful act, eg. breach of a major contract condition, injury from work-related accident, etc. Usually paid as compensation through the court.

Where a contract is breached there may be a right to repudiate it or opt out, otherwise damages may be claimed.

Data Advantage Ltd The Australia-wide agency that collects credit information on all entities that use credit. Only members may access information when selling on credit and in turn must report on defaults. A good credit reference is vital to all users of credit. Formerly the Credit Reference Association (CRA).

Members are businesses that offer credit and have paid a joining fee. Information is confidential but people or businesses may correct inaccurate information.

data control *Data* is information collected, usually through computer programs. *Control* comes from the manipulation of such data to achieve expected outcomes or results.

Use of computers in production, robotics, etc aids the presentation and control of data.

dealership An agent appointed by a principal is a dealer. Dealers are usually

For example, car dealerships appointed by car

appointed to service geographic areas or for particular periods.

manufacturers, or Harvey Norman appointed by Fisher & Paykel.

debenture **(1)** The security over all the assets of a company in return for a loan. **(2)** A debt instrument paying interest to an investor in a public debt issue.

A *fixed debenture* is a company loan over a specific asset. A *floating debenture* is over all other assets of a business.

debt Borrowings from outside the business, usually from banks, finance companies, investors, government or other finance intermediaries. Public company debt offered to the public as debentures/bonds must have a prospectus. Security is usually provided over assets.

Appears as current or non-current liabilities in the Statement of Financial Position. Interest is paid to lenders.

debt defeasance Involves the negotiation or swap of a formal debt for shares or other equity interests in a business.

Often used by venture capital companies who may forego a debt for service in favour of limited shareholding.

debtor A person or business (external entity) that owes money to a business. *See* accounts receivable.

Shows as a receivable in the Statement of Financial Position (Balance Sheet).

decision tree A diagram that shows various options leading to differing outcomes and probabilities Improves decision-making.

A decision-making tool such as Critical Path Analysis, PERT, SWOT and scheduling.

delegation The act of giving a person authority and hence responsibility for carrying out a specific task. Accountability goes with the delegation.

A senior manager who has delegated a duty may still be accountable to more senior managers.

demarcation dispute Conflict over whom should be responsible for certain work tasks.

These have traditionally been disputes between different unions.

democratic management The style of participative management based on the majority decision and usually including all staff.

Other styles may be laissez-faire, collegial, autocratic, etc.

demographic factors Population factors which may affect customer spending, eg. income levels, ethnicity, age, spending patterns.

The targeting of specific customers will determine the marketing approach.

demotion A reallocation to a lower-paid position with less responsibility.

demutualisation The conversion of a cooperative for members into a company issuing shares to its shareholders (members) based on the accumulated profits in the business.

Two examples of demutualisation are AMP and NRMA.

depreciation The loss or decline in the value of an asset through wear and tear or obsolescence. Tax authorities allow certain annual deductions of a portion of the costs of depreciable assets. May be a fixed % of the cost or a % of the written down value (WDV).

Applies to non-current (fixed) assets and shows as accumulated depreciation by way of deduction in the Statement of Financial Position (Balance Sheet).

deregistration The act of cancelling registration of an entity or other body where either a serious default or breach has occurred and the entity no longer represents its members.

May refer to a union in breach or a representative body, eg. sports club which no longer acts for its members.

deregulation The easing or removal of business constraints within the law so as

The easing of financial restrictions or lowering of

to increase business activity and encourage greater competition. Always government-led.

tariffs are examples.

derivatives Contracts or instruments whose value comes from some underlying asset or indicator, such as commodities (oil, gold, wool, cotton), equities (shares, options), currencies or from a financial index (All Ordinaries, NASDAQ) or indicator (interest rates). *See also* futures.

Products include swaps, forwards, futures, options, warrants, hedges, etc. Newer products are emerging continuously, eg. straddles, collars, etc.

devaluation Reducing the value of a nation's currency against all other currencies. Devaluation puts up the price of imports and gives exporters greater returns.

A lower Australian dollar (AUD) is a market devaluation due to its floating nature to others.

direct costs Expenses that can be easily identified as belonging to a particular product or service.

The raw materials and labour used directly in production, etc.

director A member of the Board in a company who has been appointed by the shareholders. Strict regulations to ensure the proper conduct of directors are set out in the *Corporations Law*.

There must be at least one director in a proprietary company. Directors control the company through a Board.

discount A reduction in the selling price of a product, or an amount allowed as a deduction if an account is paid early.

discounting In marketing, refers to the lowering of prices to stimulate sales. In capital markets, refers to the buying and selling of money market securities (eg. bonds, debentures) at a discounted rate, but which will give their full value if held to maturity.

A non-interest bearing security issued at a discount on face value, eg. at $90 instead of $100, which would be at a 10% discount. The holder receives $100 on maturity.

discrimination The act of treating a person or group of people differently due to race, ethnicity, gender, age, religion, marital status, social origin, sexual preference, political opinion, medical record or intellectual ability. *See also* anti-discrimination.

Anti-discrimination legislation now requires employers to treat all staff equally. Merit alone may be the discriminator.

disintermediation The removal of intermediaries from the supply chain between manufacturers and the end users/consumers in order to reduce marketing costs and allow consumers to buy more cheaply. Wholesalers and dealers now face the challenge of having to reinvent their worth to survive.

The Internet has hastened this process now that consumers may access suppliers directly. Both parties should benefit from lower costs.

dismissal The action taken by an employer to terminate the employment of an employee through poor performance or unacceptable behaviour.

Legislation requires strict procedures to ensure dismissal is justifiable.

dispute Any disagreement between two or more parties. May relate to wages, conditions, work safety, rostering, inadequate training, etc.

Grievance procedures are increasingly incorporated into business manuals.

dispute resolution process One of the methods used to find a mutual solution to a dispute between two or more parties.

Includes negotiation, mediation, arbitration, conciliation, grievance procedures, etc.

distribution The process of moving products from producers to retailers and to customers.

Includes transporting, warehousing and inventory control.

distribution expenses Those costs associated with the distribution process. Costs can include commissions paid to agents, wholesalers, etc.

Costs would include freight, postage, couriers and other transport costs.

diversification The expansion of a business into new products, services or markets not immediately identified to its prime function.

Includes modification of existing products or introduction of new ones, eg. BHP and oil.

dividend The share of company profits or the return paid to an owner of shares held in a company. Dividends are said to be 'franked' where the tax has been paid by the company. When franked they are tax free to the holder within certain tax ranges.

Usually paid by companies half-yearly when making profits. Bonus shares may also be issued.

dividend yield The dividend earnings, calculated as dividend per share divided by the current share price. Expressed as a percentage and used as a profitability/stability indicator.

Like most investments it is preferred that the rate exceed the rate of inflation.

downsizing The reduction of a business's organisational structure, divisions, workforce, product base or spread of interests.

Effects reporting relationships, number of employees and cost levels of the business.

downtime A period during which production is affected due to machinery or power failure, the labour force ceasing work or outside influences stopping certain operations. Very costly for a business.

Can be critical in certain industries which rely on continuous electronic processing.

drawdown The act of drawing an instalment from a loan on offer from an institution.

A loan of $100 000 may involve ten drawdowns of $10 000.

drawings The amount taken by an owner of a business (usually a sole trader or partnership) as an advance against potential profits.

Can be in cash or product, eg. farmers may kill their stock for home use.

due diligence The process undertaken by one company with another before entering into a formal relationship. Involves detailed investigation of the systems, accounting records, agreements and staff strengths, etc.

Always undertaken when one company seeks to take over or merge with another by mutual agreement

dumping The sale of a commodity in a foreign market at a lower price than that charged in the domestic market. This practice is decreasing due to the influence of the World Trade Organisation (WTO).

Used to establish a toehold in a new market. Can harm local industries and employment.

duty of care The obligation on all businesses to oversee the conditions in a workplace and for employees and through quality products and services.

Schools have a duty of care in supervising all playground activity.

E

earnings per share (EPS) A profitability and stability indicator for a company. Calculated as net after tax profit divided by the number of ordinary shares and options issued.

Used in public company annual reports to compare results year by year. *See also* times interest earned.

earnings before interest and tax (EBIT) Used in the calculation of the number of times interest is covered by profits, expressed as EBIT, and commonly used in annual reporting to facilitate financial analysis.

The calculation is:

$$\frac{\text{EBIT}}{\text{Interest costs}}$$

ecologically sustainable Development relating to the environment that

Poor treatment of our environment through

minimises or avoids damage, waste and degradation so that its continual use will allow production to be sustained into the future.

misuse and bad management has forced society to consider sustainability.

e-commerce Electronic commerce emerging worldwide through the supply of good, services and information over the Internet.

Customers are using the Internet more frequently for ease and cost reasons.

economic cycle World economic conditions tend to flow in cycles between 'boom' and 'bust' with extremes less pronounced as countries manage their economies more proficiently. Certain events may influence changes, eg. war.

Any analysis of the past will show such cycles over approximately 7 years. This cycle period is shortening. Also, some countries may seriously mismanage their economies.

economies of scale Savings made as a result of either increasing the volume of production or of spreading an administrative cost centre over more production units, divisions or subsidiaries. For example, transnationals are improving the standards of living in lesser-developed countries by spreading their productions through globalisation.

The merger of an airline, major corporation and communication group with differing technologies would expect cost savings, increased revenues and profits.

effective interest rate The amount of interest payable on a loan contract, including additional charges such as application costs, divided by the amount borrowed. Expressed as a percentage per annum.

Eg. Loan for $20 000 for 1 year
Application fee $400
Interest amount $1200
Effective rate = 8%

efficiency ratios Those ratios that reflect an improvement in cash flows of a business due to more efficient controls.

For example, average receivables divided by credit sales; cost of

Receivables turnover rate, inventory turnover rate and expense ratios reflect how efficient a business can be in its controls.

goods sold divided by average inventories.

EFTPOS Stands for electronic funds transfer at point of sale. Allows purchases in shops to be charged to banks or credit cards via a computer link with financial institutions.

Charging is automatic on entry from a customer's bank account or credit card.

EDI Stands for Electronic Data Interchange. The transfer of data between computers with specific communications and software links.

The advent of the Internet is the extension of this basic technology.

embargo The withholding of information or a ban on certain activities within a business or with another country until an event has occurred.

Governments may embargo budgets until they are officially released. Unions may embargo trade due to a disagreement.

employee benefits Advantages provided for staff by an employer. Include motor vehicles, health or education services, laptops, etc.

May be fringe benefits which an employer must declare to the ATO each year.

employee relations Comprises all staff-related matters such as hiring, induction, education, performance reviews, remuneration, grievance procedures, fringe benefits and counselling. Previously known as Industrial Relations.

An Employee Relations manager has a very senior role in any large business and reports directly to the Chief Executive.

employer associations Groups of employers usually representing single industries. Formed for research and to provide advice to their members.

Real Estate Institute, Motor Traders Association, Institute of Chartered Accountants, etc.

employment contract An agreement made between an employer and employee/s that defines the rights and conditions for work. Usually enforceable by law.

Can be either a union award (minimum conditions) or an enterprise agreement.

employment enrichment Programs designed to enhance employee performance, esteem, character-building, education and preparation for future roles in society.

May be internal or outside educational programs designed to build staff loyalty, teamwork etc.

empowerment The act of giving employees more authority and control over their work environment.

Results in democratic workplaces and better teamwork.

enterprise A company or business.

Also refers to having ambition or energy.

enterprise agreement An agreement between an employer and an employee or employee group which covers wages, terms and conditions of employment.

Must be approved by a court or industrial tribunal and is enforceable by law.

enterprise bargaining A decentralised process of employee negotiation and may involve unions at the option of the workforce. Negotiates wages, terms and conditions and induction requirements. Can also set minimum levels of performance for reward.

Has replaced the older union/employer negotiation with employees empowered to seek their best terms and conditions, eg. SPC agreement which provided for profit sharing.

environmental impact The effect on the environment as a result of a specific business activity. Businesses which may have an effect on the environment are required to present a report on the effects of their proposals and how they will minimise adverse impacts on the surrounding area.

Includes degradation of land, flora and fauna. Federal and State laws have established bodies to oversee environmental impact, eg. Environmental Protection Agency (EPA).

Equal Employment Opportunity (EEO) Federal legislation which ensures fair and equal work opportunities for all employees. Aimed particularly at assisting women to enter the workforce.

The intent is to seek equal pay for equal work and not disadvantage any employees in attaining their work objectives.

equity The capital and accumulated funds and reserves shown in the Statement of Financial Position (Balance Sheet) as the total of Owners' Equity or the amounts owing to external entities, including the owner. May also be an owner's share of an asset (eg. property) excluding loans. In general terms, can also mean the doctrine of fairness, equality and sharing between parties.

Also known as Owners' Equity or Shareholders' Funds. Distinct from debt which is borrowings.

equity financing The raising of finance by offering shares in a business. Shares can only be offered to the public through a prospectus issued by a public company. A small business may issue shares on commencement as a company but these have limited ability to be traded.

Shares in a public company may be ordinary, preference, cumulative preference or redeemable. All raise finance on issue and may be traded.

establishment The first stage in the commencement of a business and its life cycle.

Followed by incorporation, growth, maturity, renewal or decline and cessation.

establishment fee An amount paid to a financial institution to set up a loan facility for a business.

Will differ between institutions and may relate to an overdraft, commercial bill line, trade facilities, term loan, etc.

ethics Minimum levels of behaviour adopted in a business reflecting

Unethical behaviour is unacceptable and is distinct

society's attitudes and expectations of fairness and justice.

from illegal behaviour which is against the law.

Euro The currency adopted by the European Union (EU) as the standard unit of exchange by its member countries.

Nearly all EU members have adopted it. The UK is yet to join.

European Union The group comprising most countries within Europe. Previously the European Economic Community (EEC).

In 2001, Denmark had not yet joined. Some of the Eastern European countries await acceptance.

exchange rate The rate at which one currency can be exchanged for another when buying or selling currencies.

Rates may change daily and are quoted in newspapers.

executive summary A brief and precise outline of a more detailed report which follows. Endeavours to encapsulate the main points in no more than two pages using tables and lists. *See* p. xv.

Busy people need a short report to highlight key issues. Should state facts, options and key recommendations.

expense ratios Where individual expense items are separately divided by total sales, with each expressed as a percentage. These ratios are useful for comparison against previous years and also against industry averages. Expenses may be separate or identified by major categories, such as Administration, Finance, Marketing and Staff.

Where total sales are 100%, calculations are made for cost of goods sold and the respective expenses.

expenses Amounts spent by a business for goods or services in earning revenues. Expenses appear in the Statement of Financial Performance (Revenue Statement or Profit & Loss Account) as costs deducted from revenues to determine profits.

Rent, wages, phones, bank fees and car costs are examples. Require approval before payment to suppliers.

exporting The sending of goods overseas for promotion and sale. Requires knowledge of international cultures, import regulations and currencies.

Expertise may be offered through services to overseas users.

export licence Document required before certain goods can be exported from a country.

For example, armaments, native plants, animals, etc.

external environment Those factors outside a business that can influence its direction.

Legal, governmental, economic and global events may impact.

F

factoring The sale by a business of its accounts receivable to a financial institution. The financier can provide a range of service options such as full ledger administration, credit evaluation, control and collection, marketing assistance, sales analysis and customer counselling. Liaison between factor and client is continual and the collection rate can influence the fee. Export factors offer full international services. The business turnover is not constrained through financial restrictions. Highly recommended for growth businesses.

The purchase may be up to 85% with the balance held as a retention. The fee will depend upon the services offered. Full service plus credit risk may be around 2–3%, subject to the type of business and collection rate. The fee is a combination of finance charge, administration and credit risk fee.

family friendly programs Initiatives where businesses provide working environments to suit employees with families.

Includes work rosters for mothers and provision of creche facilities.

feedback controls Communication with customers regarding the quality of the product or service, with deficiencies being fixed.

May involve customer surveys and product reviews in target markets.

feedforward controls *See* prevention controls.

fibre optics Bundles of fine glass threads which can conduct information through light. A new technology which is fast and carries tremendous loads of data.

Has revolutionised global communications and the growth of the Internet.

FIFO The system of inventory management that moves inventory on a 'first in first out' basis. This may mean the cost of goods equates more to the earliest values or older inventory which may be less than present values. The gross profit would then be marginally more.

See also LIFO and HIFO.

fiduciary duty The duty of directors to act in good faith and in the company's interests at all times, and to avoid conflicts of interest.

These obligations are included in the *Corporations Law.*

finance companies Businesses that accept investor monies and lend to business and personal borrowers. Usually offer a range of finance types including leasing, factoring and trade finance. *See* p. xvii.

Major finance companies include AGC and GE Capital. Finance costs a little more than bank financing.

finance lease Where an asset owned by another is rented by a user who pays the owner a regular amount. A finance lease usually has a residual lump sum which, if paid on completion, will give the purchaser ownership. *See also* operating lease.

Finance leases are non-cancellable. Payments are deductible for tax, and the asset and the liability remaining must appear in the Statement of Financial Position (Balance Sheet).

financial controls Involves the use of budgets, comparisons with actual results, receivables and inventory checking for cash flow efficiency.

Cost control and proper authorising of expenses is vital.

financial expenses The costs of a business related to interest, leasing, factoring, bank fees and guarantee costs.

Show on the Statement of Financial Performance along with Administration, Marketing and Staff Costs.

financial forecasts Predictions of product revenues, total expenditures by category, profits, capital expenditure and staff needs in monetary terms. Included in the business plan. *See* p. xv.

Also known as budgets for comparing actual performance. Also include cash flow forecasts.

financial indicators Management reports that show profitability, cash flows, comparative financial ratios, productivity, budgets to actual results. Show the status of the business in the Statements of Financial Performance and Position (Balance Sheet).

See also non-financial indicators.

financial instruments Shares, debentures, commercial bills, bonds, government securities, derivatives contracts, asset-backed bonds and so on.

Able to be traded for listed companies.

financial intermediaries People and businesses which trade in the capital markets on behalf of others, or which provide advisory services between lenders and borrowers.

Examples are banks, stockbrokers, investment banks, advisors, money market operators or finance companies.

financial markets The conglomerate of financial institutions and investors who invest and trade in money securities,

Financial markets include both buyers and sellers.

including the ASX, primary and secondary capital markets, money market dealers, stockbrokers, banks, finance groups and investment banks.

financial ratios *See* Important financial ratios on p. xi.

financial stability The status of a business that is generating sufficient profits to pay lenders and owners yet still retain earnings for growth.

See also ratio analysis and the stability ratios on p. xiii.

fixed assets Comprise property assets, owned motor vehicles, plant and equipment, furniture, fittings and patents. Shown in the Statement of Financial Position (Balance Sheet).

Known as capital assets or non-current assets on which a business generates its income and which are depreciated annually.

fixed costs Overhead expenses that do not change with increases in volume of business activity. Appear in the Statement of Financial Performance (Revenue Statement or Profit & Loss Account).

Typical examples are rent, airconditioning and heating. Distinct from variable costs.

fixed rates Usually interest rates that are guaranteed not to change for a specific period of a loan. Business and home borrowers will select a suitable option. Fixed rates are generally higher than variable rates.

May revert to variable or be converted by borrower election. Normally variable rates are 0.5–0.75% lower.

flat rate interest A rate of interest charged on an amount borrowed and multiplied by the number of years the loan is outstanding. No longer used, but replaced with a more honest 'effective rate'.

See also effective interest rate.

flattened management structure A system of business organisation where more subordinates report to a management which has fewer levels. Up to 15 managers may report to a Chief Executive.

The pyramid structure often had few reporting but many more levels and is being largely superceded by the flattened structure.

float **(1)** The promotion of a new issue of shares or debentures in a public company in the primary capital market. **(2)** The action in a currency market to allow currencies to move according to market conditions.

A public float requires a prospectus to be issued.

floating debenture The security given over all the assets of a business to a lender for loans made.

Distinct from a specific debenture given over a selected asset.

force-field analysis A technique used to examine the forces which are helping, resisting or hindering advancement from a current position to a desired one.

foreign debt The accumulated amount owed by government, the financial markets, business and private trading enterprises in one country to other countries' financial institutions. Overseas borrowing carries an exchange risk.

Foreign debt will fluctuate with exchange rates. Countries often talk of 'per cent to GDP' when making comparisons.

foreign exchange market Where currencies are traded by financial institutions acting for buyers and sellers.

Banks and investment banks are the major participants.

foreign exchange risk When buying or selling goods for a price expressed in an overseas currency, the foreign exchange risk occurs when the exchange rates alter

Businesses will commonly use forward cover, hedging contracts or will pay from overseas accounts to reduce risk.

at the time of repayment. A borrower will then face a currency profit or loss.

forward cover A foreign exchange contract between an Australian bank and a customer under which the bank agrees to buy or sell a fixed amount in overseas currency on a nominated date at the rate of exchange in the contract. Banks are ethically obligated to ensure borrowers in overseas currencies are advised of the risks.

Used by most businesses which borrow overseas and do not have overseas accounts. Bank loans in foreign currency to farmers in the 1980s doubled when the exchange rate moved against them and no forward cover was in place.

Four P's The major variables considered by business in achieving its market objectives: product, price, promotion and place.

Preparation of a marketing plan will require detailed consideration of each. *See also* product, price, promotion, place.

franchise A method of marketing where a well-known brand or product and name is licensed for sale to another for a fee.

McDonalds, The Body Shop, Jim's Mowing, House & Garden and Bakers Delight are examples.

franked dividends The return paid to shareholders where the company has paid the tax. Dividends may also be partially franked.

These are tax-free to the recipient to the extent of their franking.

freehold Where an owner may hold a property until its title is sold to another. *See also* leasehold.

Owners may do as they wish subject to any local council laws.

fringe benefit A non-wage/salary benefit often incorporated into a remuneration package. It is subject to a fringe benefits tax payable to the ATO by the business at quarterly intervals.

Examples are health care, education, overseas travel, motor vehicles, laptops and certain defined entertainment.

functional management System in which line managers (those reporting to seniors) delegate authority over subordinates to a staff manager, eg. a support service function.

For example, a quality control person is given authority to report to an Employee Relations Manager.

funds statement Documents the source and application of funds for a business, eg. where money has come from and where it has gone. The Statement of Cash Flows has replaced this.

Public companies rarely report in this older format.

futures (contract) When an agreement to buy or sell delivery of a specified commodity is exchanged and the parties complete them at a later date at the price determined in the contract. Often negotiated through a futures exchange (SFE/ASX). Risky without a sound knowledge. Also known as a derivative.

May cover currencies, commodities, interest rates, etc, where a contract may safeguard against paying a higher price for a commodity later.

G

Gantt chart A scheduling tool presented as a bar graph with time and activities shown on the two axes.

Similar to critical path analysis, PERT and decision trees.

gearing (leverage) ratio The relationship of external liabilities (debt) to owners' equity. The ratio is a measure of the stability or solvency of a business. The higher the debt, the less solvent the business and the higher the risk for creditors.

The ratio is:

$$\frac{\text{Total liabilities}}{\text{Owners' equity}}$$

A small business with total liabilities greater than owners' equity will face difficulty.

generic brand An in-house product packed or prepared for a specific outlet. Usually cheaper and identified to the outlet.

May be branded as identified to the outlet, eg. Woolworths has Home Brand, Coles has Farmland.

glass ceiling A perceived or artificial barrier to women advancing into more senior roles in business and society.

The participation rate is increasing as more women take up career opportunities.

globalisation The movement to include all countries in trade and other extending services. Facilitated by transnationals and emerging technologies such as communications.

Intended to enhance world trade and decrease poverty in less developed countries.

going concern A business that is expected to continue operations into the future.

Its worth as a going concern would be greater than its break-up value.

Goods and Services Tax (GST) The 10% tax introduced in 2000 added to goods and services at all stages of production. Ultimately paid by the final consumer. Certain items are GST-free, eg. basic foods.

See also BAS and PAYG as related features.

goodwill An intangible asset showing on a Statement of Financial Position (Balance Sheet) which may arise through its ability to generate higher than normal profits. May have a unique customer base which has real value or is the current worth of expected future profits. Can also arise as the monetary difference (premium or discount) between the price

Appears as an intangible asset with patents, trademarks, logos, etc. Often an amount incorporated in a merger. Can be written off over a period.

paid for a business and the value of the net assets acquired after purchase.

go-slow A situation where employees purposely work slowly to bring management action on a grievance.

Frequently used in industrial disputes over workers' wages and conditions.

Government Business Enterprise (GBE) A business or company owned and operated by the government. May be the stage before privatisation, or established to put the government organisation on a profit objective.

Often a move by government to commercialise an operation before privatising.

Government securities Treasury notes or Federal and State Government-issued bonds.

Issued for terms up to 10 years and traded in capital markets.

grievance procedures A series of steps outlined in an industry award or set out in the induction manual of a progressive business which aims to minimise and settle major disruptions or disputes.

A responsibility of the Employment Relations Manager who usually reports to the Chief Executive.

Gross Domestic Product (GDP) The total output of business and government sectors in a period which indicates the level of economic activity in the country.

An important measure of business and economic management.

gross profit/loss Shown in the Statement of Financial Performance (Revenue Statement or Profit & Loss Statement) as revenues less cost of goods sold (COGS). A gross loss occurs where COGS exceeds revenues.

Cost of goods sold is Opening inventories + purchases and direct freight costs – closing inventories.

gross profit ratio A profitability ratio where gross profit is divided by total

It is usual that a high turnover business will have

sales and expressed as a percentage. Lowering the COGS may improve the gross profit, as will a greater mark-up.

a lower gross profit % than, for example, a jeweller with a lower turnover.

growth A stage in the life cycle of a business, evidenced by increasing sales, an expanded target market and improving profitability and financial ratios. Growth may flatten out, leading to maturity. This is a time for renewal or decline.

Follows establishment stages of a business, or may follow renewal where a business has restructured and revitalised its products.

guarantee **(1)** A commitment given by one party to answer for the debt of another. Works when the primary debtor fails and the guarantee then is called upon. **(2)** An assurance by a manufacturer that any faulty products will be remedied within a certain period.

Is a form of collateral given to support a loan. It is a common ethic in practice that a guarantee will not make a doubtful loan good.

H

hedging contract A contract used by traders in futures and foreign exchange markets to protect themselves against price or exchange rate variations and thereby reduce risk.

A form of insurance. Markets offer hedging contracts on various products, eg. gold, interest rates, currencies and even live cattle.

HIFO The system of inventory management that moves inventory on a 'highest in first out' basis. This may mean the cost of goods taken into production would be the highest in inventory and therefore the gross profit may be marginally less.

See also LIFO and FIFO.

hire-purchase The acquisition of an asset by paying a financial institution equal instalments of principle and interest over a specified period. Legal (as distinct from physical) possession did not pass until the final payment was made. The chattel mortgage system now allows possession to pass when most of the debt has been met but payment by instalment still applies. *See also* chattel mortgage.

Also known as time payment and the newer term, chattel mortgage.

historic cost A convention whereby capital assets (eg. property, plant and equipment) are shown in the Statement of Financial Position (Balance Sheet) at their original cost over time.

Directors may revalue a property held for some time to reflect its true and current value.

hits The number of times a web page is accessed on the Internet. A record of interest to website administrators.

The user is often identified to the site administrator for potential sales.

holding company A company which owns over 50% of the shares in another company or companies. The other companies are known as *subsidiaries*.

Sometimes referred to as a 'parent' company. A company with 20% or more of its share owned by another company is known as a *controlled entity*.

horizontal integration The merger or integration of companies or businesses producing similar products or services, eg. if Woolworths acquires some Franklin stores.

Distinct from *vertical integration* which brings in a company or business at a different level of the production chain.

Human Resources (HR) management The policies and activities of a division to oversee employees in all aspects of their

Involves staff acquisition, development, induction, motivation, remuneration, employment. Now renamed Employment Relations as an update of current practices. The range of duties in this role is substantial. Note the recent trend for large companies to outsource some roles.

performance appraisal, organisational objectives, grievance handling, etc.

I

idle time Time during which employees or plant is inactive. May be the result of breakdowns, disputes or planned maintenance.

Unplanned idle time can be very expensive where processes are continuous and automated.

implied terms Terms of a contract which may not have been discussed or written but have been understood from the behaviour of the parties.

A purchase is implied when shoppers put goods in a shopping trolley.

imputation The process of a company paying tax on dividends on behalf of its shareholders. Such tax is said to be imputed.

Also is the rate of interest imputed as applying to non-interest bearing investments for welfare entitlements.

incentive Something that encourages a person to do something better. Can be a component of a remuneration package or reward.

May be a promotion, monetary reward or fringe benefit offered for meeting certain performance criteria.

income Revenues from sales, rent and interest received. *See also* revenue.

incorporation The process by which a company is formed and registered as a legal entity via a Certificate of

Processed through ASIC, the body which also supervises the company's

Incorporation. Follows establishment when a business gets bigger and seeks to restrict personal liability. A stage in the life cycle of a business.

statutory obligations.

in the money The term used in financial markets to refer to an options contract that can be exercised to give a profit. *At the money* means the exercise price will give neither a profit nor loss, and *out of the money* means the contract would give a loss.

indirect costs Expenses which cannot directly be identified to production. Normally known as overheads which are recorded in the Statement of Financial Performance (Revenue Statement or Profit & Loss Account).

Can be administration, marketing, finance and staff expenses. Also include certain tax obligations, eg. fringe benefits tax.

induction The process of introducing new staff to a work environment. Includes introduction of a business's culture, products or services, employment terms and conditions and related policies. Often presented as a manual for use and study.

Many businesses now include a change charter in their induction manuals. The Internet is facilitating company induction programs.

Industrial Court The court that hears cases involving businesses, unions, employers and employees.

May also be delegated to a specialist industrial tribunal.

inflation The increase in the prices of goods and services in a country. Usually measured by the Consumer Price Index (CPI). Most countries seek to minimise extremes in economic activity, although world trade cycles will continue.

A high inflation rate will impair a country's economic progress and may lead to extreme cycle variations in economic activity.

I

information superhighway General term describing the vast network of communications devices which provide extensive and diverse knowledge to homes and businesses using computers.

Transmitted through radio, satellite, microwave, optic fibre, cable mediums, etc.

information technology (IT) The branch of a business responsible for systems, data capture, communications, reporting, analysis, Management Information Systems (MIS) and any computer-related matters.

Large businesses have extensive IT divisions. Their importance usually requires reporting to the Chief Executive.

injunction A specific order by a court directing one party in a dispute to refrain from doing an act which another party has opposed.

Where employers and employees are in negotiations, a threat of industrial action may cause an injunction to be issued to prevent it.

innovation A new idea or method of doing something normally done another way. For a business to continue to succeed, innovation should be encouraged. Often used as an incentive for staff to improve on existing procedures or methods of presentation.

It is predicted that the life of a product is around 10 years unless constant innovation has maintained its market.

input tax credit Where GST has been added to purchases, it may be claimed as an input tax credit against GST collected on supplies (sales) when calculating a business obligation in the Business Activity Statement (BAS). Can also be cash claimed back from the ATO where the input tax credits are greater than the GST collected.

See also GST, PAYG, BAS.

insider trading The practice of a person or institution associated with the Board or management of a listed company (or who acts in an advisory capacity to the company) trading in the company shares when they have prior knowledge of a situation from which they will benefit.

Listed companies are obligated to advise the ASX of any information that may impact on the listed share price. Insider trading is illegal and subject to strict penalties.

insolvency The inability of a business to pay its debts as they arise. It is illegal for a company to continue to trade when insolvent, and directors may become personally liable.

When the current ratio (CA/CL) is less than 1:1 the business may be in a cash crisis or, in extreme cases, insolvent.

insurance A policy taken out with an insurance company or broker that on payment of a sum of money (premium), a certain protection will be afforded. Small businesses should carry fire, motor vehicle, plant and equipment, loss of profit, burglary and product liability insurance.

Typically, insurance would be taken by large businesses for fire, loss of profits, directors' and officers' liability and product liability.

intangible assets Valuable resources that are shown in the Statement of Financial Position (Balance Sheet). Include goodwill, trademarks, patents, copyrights and logos. Can be written off progressively.

Show as intangible assets, a group of assets below non-current assets.

intellectual property Ownership of ideas, new methods, research work or any other matter that has been developed by an individual or business and has value. Includes copyrights and logos.

Such property is capable of protection and owners may take legal action if another party has assumed ownership.

interactive television The technology which allows users to access a range of

The personal computer may surrender some use to

features through their television screens, such as watching various channels, accessing Internet sites for shopping, banking or other business functions, knowledge, games (single or multi-player) and telephone access.

cordless access to TV sets through datacasting and digital television services.

interest rate The price, expressed as a percentage per annum, for borrowing or lending money.

The capital markets can influence this based on the base interest rate set by the Reserve Bank from time to time.

interest rate swaps The exchange of a fixed interest rate for a variable or floating rate by way of a swap contract. A business may have borrowed where the rate or term is now inappropriate whereas another business may have a need.

A contract negotiated by banks, money market dealers, futures traders or directly by the parties so that each should benefit from the result.

intermediaries Persons acting between parties. May be wholesalers between manufacturers and customers, or stockbrokers acting for two businesses. *See also* disintermediation.

Any participant in the capital markets may act as an intermediary between parties.

internal audit A division within a business appointed to check adherence to procedures, finances and the correctness of record-keeping and reporting. Assists the external auditor (external audit firms must be appointed by public companies annually).

The responsibility for company management in a public company is prioritised as follows: directors/officers; auditors; ASIC or other supervisory body. Directors must meet certain statutory requirements.

internal environment Refers to factors within the business such as location, staff, its products, services and other internal activities.

internal rate of return (IRR) The rate of return on an investment calculated by finding the discount rate that compares the present value of future cash flows to the total cost of the investment.

Other evaluation methods include payback, accounting rate of return, discounted cash flow and net present value.

International Labour Organisation (ILO) The peak international union body resident in Geneva, Switzerland. The ACTU is a member.

Coordinates actions between member countries where disputes may affect members in any country.

International Monetary Fund (IMF) A specialist agency of the UN established in 1945 to make loans to countries for basic infrastructure projects. Promotes foreign exchange stability, orderly trade and the liquidity of financial markets.

The general liquidity of financial markets is important for world trade and political stability.

inventories Goods on hand or purchased by a business for the purpose of sale at a profit. Include raw materials, work-in-progress and finished goods which have not yet been sold. Also known as *stocks*.

Inventories are shown under current assets in the Statement of Financial Position. The closing inventory is also a component of COGS.

inventory control Ensuring that inventory types are available as required by the business or its customers while also ensuring that costs are minimised in storage, finance and out-of-date items. Just-in-Time techniques are used to minimise inventories.

Just-in-Time is the control technique where regular reorders are triggered when minimum stocks are held, allowing for the transit time.

inventory turnover ratio An efficiency ratio where the cost of goods sold is

The rate of annual inventory turnover will

divided by the average of opening and closing inventories. The difference from one year to another will reflect the level of efficiency of a business in turning inventory over more times a year.

depend on the type of business, eg. for a jeweller may be three times while a fruiterer may be 310 times a year.

investment bank A bank which deals with business, investments, foreign trade, currencies, derivatives, underwriting and financial advisory services. A major participant in the capital markets. The more acceptable name for merchant banks.

Usually has very strong parentage and global connections. Large deal maker.

investments The investment of money into either a capital asset to generate revenue through production and sale, or from an interest return Capital assets such as property and plant and equipment are productive assets, which generate the inventory.

Investments in inventories or marketable securities when able to be converted into cash within 12 months are current assets.

Internet Service Provider (ISP) A business that provides the link between users and the Internet via a server.

Examples are Telstra BigPond, OzEmail and iPrimus.

J

job analysis **(1)** The analysis of a position (job) into categories of its relevant duties, level of skill required and attributes required of an employee to meet performance criteria. *See also* skills analysis. **(2)** The skills required for particular tasks within a business.

Undertaken when a total review of the skills held within a business is being done or when new tasks are being considered and a position description is being prepared.

job description *See* position description.

job enrichment The process of making jobs more satisfying and motivational by training and building identifiable responsibilities, the potential for achievement and recognition into each task.

Involves the building of teamwork, loyalty, innovation and excitement giving a desirable outcome.

job evaluation **(1)** The process of comparing jobs and the aptitudes and technical qualities required to perform a job's tasks. **(2)** A performance review of how well a person has performed in their allocated tasks.

Performance reviews may lead to a number of outcomes, eg. more training, promotion in the organisation or higher remuneration.

job satisfaction The level of enjoyment and fulfilment in a job. Staff performance, teamwork, idea generation, positive attitude to tasks and empathy with others are all key factors. The treatment of staff is important.

Personality differences can be a distraction to satisfaction. Remuneration is a vital component.

job-sharing Where a job is allocated to more than one person or where differing people are employed at different times to do the same task.

joint venture A contractual arrangement where two or more parties undertake an economic activity subject to joint control.

All parties involved in major activities must give consent.

Just-in-Time (JIT) A manual or computerised software program used to reorder inventory to ensure its arrival in time for production. The intent is to minimise inventory levels and avoid high inventory finance costs and potential obsolescence.

A modern technique in inventory control and quality reviews to maximise funds use.

K

kaizen The Japanese concept of constantly seeking improvement and questioning the status quo in quality control.

Edward Deming, an American, first advocated quality control in Japan in 1946.

key management roles The senior positions within a business. A Chief Executive Officer (CEO) is the most senior in a large business. If the CEO is also a director he/she may be the Managing Director. A small business manager may be a General Manager. An organisation structure is normally set out as a chart showing the relationship between senior staff and their subordinates. The higher the level on the chart, the more senior the position.

Reporting to the senior executive may be divisional managers or support service managers, eg. Financial Controller, Marketing Manager, Production Manager or Employment Relations Manager.

L

labour market The society in which people seek work, employers offer work, skills are learned and improved. Remuneration is determined by bargaining between people with certain skills and employers in this market. It is a place where people do tasks that match their ambitions. A vital economic indicator of government effort, usually reported quarterly.

When unemployment as a percentage of the labour force is too high, it may reflect a world downturn or poor economic management.

labour on-costs The additional costs of employing people which have to be counted as incurred or potential costs. Such costs can be up to 30% above the direct remuneration rate.

Include long service and annual leave, fringe benefits tax, payroll tax, superannuation, sick pay, dress allowances and workers compensation.

laissez-faire A style of management where employees set and implement their own goals with minimum supervision. Suited to creative work environments.

French term for 'allow to act'.

large business Defined in the *Corporations Law* as being a business that has a large market share, a turnover exceeding $10 million and total assets over $5 million.

May be a proprietary or public company. Usually has a complex structure and is divisionalised.

leading Where the senior manager projects a vision of where the business is going in the short and long term, and directs and motivates employees to achieve the organisation's objectives.

A component of the management function often referred to as the POLC model, ie. planning, organising, leading and controlling.

lead time **(1)** The time between placement of a reorder of inventory and the time of its arrival from a supplier. **(2)** The time between commencement of a production run and completion of the product.

leasehold Where a real property owner (landlord) contracts to allow use of a property by another party (tenant) under a temporary agreement. *See also* freehold.

Frequently under fixed periods where the landlord continues to pay rates but not electricity.

lease A contract between an owner who has purchased an asset and retains

Usually motor vehicles, plant and equipment,

L

ownership and a user who rents it for a period and pays a lease fee. A *finance lease* has a residual value and is usually non-cancellable, whereas an *operating lease* (also *leveraged lease*) is cancelleable and more of a rental.

furniture, computers, etc. The presentation in a Statement of Financial Position (Balance Sheet) is different for each type.

lessee The hirer (or tenant, in the case of property) under a lease agreement.

lessor The owner of the asset hired under a lease agreement, eg. landlord for a property.

letter of offer A letter sent to a successful applicant for a position setting out the terms and conditions of an offer of employment.

Would normally require the return of an acknowledg-ment or acceptance.

level playing field A situation where all parties face equal pressures from the business environment, giving a measure of equality that is fair to all parties.

Competition may allow one party to have a competitive advantage.

leverage ratio *See* gearing ratio.

leveraged lease A lease arrangement where the lessor arranges for other debt and equity partners to participate in financing the cost of the asset for lease.

For example, some State authorities have sold and leased back coal-fired power plants.

liabilities What a business owes to external entities. Shown as current or non-current liabilities in the Statement of Financial Position (Balance Sheet).

Usually accounts payable, commercial bills, bank overdrafts or term loans and mortgages on property.

LIFO The system of inventory management that moves inventory on a 'last in first out' basis. This may mean

Management has a choice as to which method will be used when taking

the cost of goods taken into production would be the value of the last component entered into inventory and may be higher than the average of all components. The gross profit may be marginally less.

components from stock into production. *See also* FIFO, HIFO.

limited liability company A company which has been registered with ASIC and the liability of shareholders is limited to the paid-up or uncalled portion of any share capital.

Sole traders and partnerships can lose their possessions in the event of failure of their business.

line authority The power given by the Board of a large business to the management, or by the owner of a smaller business to the personnel responsible for running the business. Gives the power to make decisions and direct subordinates in the chain of command.

liquidity The possession of adequate cash resources to meet financial obligations when they fall due or as obligations arise. The level of liquidity in a business is an indication of its short-term financial stability.

Often measured by use of the current ratio CA/CL. The measure of how quickly an asset may be cashed.

liquidity ratios Those ratios that identify the measure of liquidity in any business. *See* the liquidity ratios on p. xi.

Current ratio and liquid/quick asset ratio apply.

liquid asset (acid test) ratio The ratio of current assets less inventory divided by current liabilities less bank overdraft. If assets are much less than liabilities it indicates cash flow problems for the business.

A liquidity ratio vital in indicating the extent to which a business has limited or adequate cash.

L

liquidation The process of winding up the affairs of a business, selling its assets and paying its creditors according to their priorities. Administration usually precedes liquidation. The *Corporations Law* sets out the process for such an action.

A business may be placed 'under administration' to endeavour to trade out of its difficulties first. Accountants are appointed to act.

list price The usual or regular price of a good before any discount or reduction is made.

listed company A public company that has been listed on a stock exchange. Listed companies can facilitate trading in their securities, and raise capital and loans by issuing shares or debentures to the general public by prospectus.

In Australia, listed on the Australian Stock Exchange (ASX); in the USA, on the New York Stock Exchange (NYSE), where the daily quotes are on the 'Dow'

litigation The taking of legal action by one party against another in a court. If substantial in a business, any litigation should be disclosed as a contingent liability in the Statement of Financial Position (Balance Sheet).

Can be expensive to proceed or defend and may require a provision in the accounts.

loan maturity The date a loan made by a financial institution is due to be repaid by a borrower.

Treasury notes, bonds and debentures also have maturity dates for redemption.

location The place where a business has based its operation. Depends on various factors, eg. availability of labour, raw materials and support services, nearness to markets, cost of leasing or property purchase, government regulations and adequate communications (phone, Internet, etc).

There may be personal reasons such as family, relations, climate, lifestyle.

lockout The action taken by an employer to refuse admission to a workplace due to a dispute or health and safety issue.

loss leader Usually a high volume sales product which is priced very competitively or at a small loss to bring in other sales with better margins.

Commonly used by supermarkets.

M

macroeconomics The functioning of the economy on an aggregate or national basis. Concerned with aggregate income, expenditure, investment, saving, inflation, unemployment and balance of payments.

Looks at the 'big picture'.

macro environment Includes economic, legal, political, social and technological factors that influence a business. The macro environment may dictate the development of the corporate culture by management.

management **(1)** The coordination of the financial, human, physical, information resources and specialist skills in an ethical, caring and innovative environment so as to achieve the short- and long-term objectives of the business. **(2)** The team of senior managers with subordinates in a business.

The manner in which the owners seek to establish their style with staff sets the corporate culture of the business. The PDLC planning model is an aid for management.

management by objectives (MBO) An older theory of management involving the development of objectives for key areas or divisions at all levels and the measuring of progress and results. Currently out of favour.

Requires empathy with staff at all levels and good guidance to address issues. The business's achievements measures the degree of success.

management information systems (MIS) Mainly computer-based systems that link all divisions in a business. Help decision-making by communicating information between areas.

Regular reporting of a business's progress can highlight deviations for early correction.

management styles These have tended to change over time from autocratic (with constant supervision) to more democratic (encouraging employee empowerment). *See also* collegial, laissez-faire.

Leaders today are motivators, coaches, mentors and good communicators with people skills.

management theories Philosophies which seek to explain how businesses should be managed to obtain objectives most effectively.

Examples are classical, behavioural, MBO, quantitative, systems, value added, democratic, TQM.

manufacturing The process of transforming material resources into a product, utilising technology and labour.

A complex combination of diverse inputs that ensure products meet customer wants.

margin The proportion of the costing intended to recover both expenses of the business and contribute a profit. *See also* mark-up.

Gross profit margins are often higher in service-based businesses.

market capitalisation The value applied to the number of shares in a listed public company multiplied by the present ASX market value.

When market prices fall, the media often refer to market capitalisation causing a business to crash.

market forecast Prediction of prices and volumes for the demand for a given product or service.

Used when a business is targeting a market or starting a promotional campaign.

market niche A segment of a total market which offers a particular advantage for the promotion of a product or service.

Defined by demographics such as age of customers, wealth, etc.

market penetration The extent to which a product or service has penetrated a market. Expressed as an actual market share percentage.

A market may be saturated/flooded with goods, eg. mobile phones.

market research The systematic collecting and analysis of information from a marketplace in order to establish a business strategy for promotion of a product or service.

Reviews competition, distribution networks, market outlets, socio-economic customer base, etc.

market segmentation *See* market niche.

market share Expressed as a percentage of an available market for a particular product or service. For example, where the total market is 100%, the share held by Company X may be 6.5%.

Market share is often used as a financial objective for annual business planning, eg. to increase the market share of a product from 4% to 8%.

market value The current price at which an asset is held or the current price at which a security is traded.

Price will be determined by valuation or trade.

marketing The coordination of activities that determine the product, price, promotion and place (the Four P's) for a product or service. The aim is to meet a business's objectives through satisfying customer needs and wants. Innovation is a key ingredient.

Involves situational analysis, SWOT, research, distribution systems, warehousing, innovative product packaging and promotions.

M

marketing mix *See* Four P's.

marketing objectives Statements of what is to be achieved through marketing activities.

For example, what product sales, market share, profit, etc.

marketing plan Incorporated into the business plan and includes product base, target markets, the Four P's (product, price, promotions and place), timetable and responsibility for performance.

Marketing plans are preceded by research, a SWOT analysis amd a study of the competition.

marketing strategy A detailed written program and timetable covering the methods and support details the business will apply in meeting its marketing objectives. Options such as market penetration, product enhancement and development, market extension, diversification, cost leadership and differentiation and niche focus may be available.

Strategies will change due to competition, product changes and customer preferences. International strategies may change with instability in the market, exchange rates and credit risks, etc. SWOT analysis is strategic.

mark-up **(1)** The amount added to production costs to recover overheads, other expenses and the profit amount required. **(2)** The difference between the cost of production and the selling price.

If the production costs were $10 and the mark-up for sale was $3, then the mark-up is 30%.

mass marketing The saturation effect of an advertising or promotion program in any market.

For example, the promotion of the GST tax.

mass market The market in which consumers find products that have been produced in such volume that product differentiation is difficult.

Products such as milk, bread, sugar, flour and other staple products.

mass production The manufacture of large quantities of identical products, usually of low cost, that do not require individual craftsmanship, eg. soft drink or milk containers.

Programmed CAD/CAM technology (robotics) has simplified this process.

maturity In the life cycle of a business, maturity is the stage where a business is well-known, has a good product, produces satisfactory profits and steady sales, and has a good reputation.

The other stages are establishment, growth, decline or post-maturity, renewal, crisis and cessation.

measures of business success Generally, these would be continuing profits, growing product base and sales, good market share, hard-working and loyal staff with opportunities for advancement, quality products and an extensive customer base.

Managers with experience in business are innovative, have good people and decision-making skills, are open to change and give clear directions.

mediation The process involving an independent third party assisting two or more parties to solve a dispute and find a solution acceptable to all.

Now a required step before parties seek the intervention of a court.

Memorandum of Association A document which sets out the name of a company, the initial subscribers to the capital, its registered office address and its major activity. Now replaced by a new document, the Constitution, and includes the Articles of Association.

A document supported by the Articles of Association which set out rules for running the company.

mens rea The legal principle of 'a guilty mind'. An intention to commit a criminal act.

merchant bank *See* investment bank.

M

merchantable quality The state that goods for sale are expected to be in: fit for their purpose and free from defects.

Also depends on the description and the circumstances of the purchase.

merger The joining together of two or more entities by mutual agreement of the shareholders or owners. Implies a degree of equality, eg. BHP and Billiton.

Usually carried out after negotiation and shareholder approval. As distinct from a takeover, which may be hostile.

microeconomics The workings of individual components of an economy in isolation. Concerned with the output of industries, prices of products and competition, and the income of households.

Growth, competition, living standards, productivity, technology uptake and innovation are examples.

middle management The level of management between top management and the workplace. There may be a number of levels in a large business. Middle levels are progressively being reduced as business seeks greater efficiency and empathy with its staff.

Businesses with many levels of management will often have frustrated employees and inadequate communications.

misappropriation The taking of money or other assets of a business for personal use when they do not belong to the user.

A serious offence usually followed by dismissal and a possible criminal charge.

mismanagement Poor administration of a business leading to crisis or failure. Generally due to inadequate knowledge of financial, marketing or people matters. Good managers will forecast most eventualities that may adversely affect a business.

Surveys of failed businesses highlight poor finance and administrative skills, and a failure to outsource as common areas of weakness.

misrepresentation An untrue statement by a vendor intended to entice a buyer to enter into a contract. Heavy penalties apply to wrongdoers.

ASIC has a role to protect buyers and prevent such actions.

mission statement A brief statement made by a business encapsulating its prime purpose and intent, usually within a 1–3 year time frame.

Supported by annual objectives. Note that a *vision statement* is a more long-term document.

mitigation The giving of a plausible reason for doing something in an effort to lessen, minimise or reduce the possible outcome of a questionable action.

In mitigation, 'I didn't know' may be the excuse!

monitoring Continually reviewing and acting on information. Involves checking, supervising and overviewing procedures or results for possible action.

Effective managers monitor marketing results from sales and advertising.

monthly statements Sent out by a business each month end to show customers their current status. Shows invoices issued for purchases each month, the amount due and overdue and any discount that may be available.

Vital function in the credit and collection policy of a business. Monthly statements also seek overdues or threaten to terminate credit facilities.

mortgage The security given over land or buildings for (usually) long-term loans. A *debenture mortgage* is a security given over either specific assets held by a company (fixed charge) or all the assets of a company (floating charge).

As distinct from *chattel mortgage* which relates to the hire-purchase of an asset.

motivation The energy, direction, purpose and effort displayed by people in their activities. Motivated employees can enhance business profits.

Motivators may be incentives, eg. money, conditions, travel or other types of reward.

M

multilateral trade agreements Agreements between two or more countries where quotas, tariffs, dumping of specific products or any other impediment to trade may be abolished or lessened. Now monitored by the World Trade Organisation (WTO).

Members of trade blocks such as the EU, ASEAN and NAFTA encourage trade between their members through special conditions subject to the WTO.

multinationals A trading entity that has a production operation in more than one country for various reasons. Multinationals, also known as transnationals seek out opportunities to enhance their profits as well as improve the standards of living in less developed countries.

Globalisation has expanded due to the WTO, transnationals, communications, improved technologies and the benefits seen for poorer countries.

multiskilling The training of people so they can competently perform a number of different tasks within a business. Previously employees were competent in a specific skill and work was passed to another skill area. This led to demarcation problems. Employees then learned other related tasks and became more flexible.

A multiskilled workforce allows more skills to be learned, more value and variety for employees and less cause for dispute.

N

national debt The total amount owed by the Federal, State and other semi-government authorities of a country. Australia's exceeds A$200 billion.

Gross national debt will always reflect the exchange rate applied on the day.

national wage case The hearing before a full bench of the Australian Industrial

The result will affect Federal awards. State

Relations Commission (AIRC) of arguments brought forward by government, unions and employer groups about minimum wage rates and conditions that should relate to awards. Usually reviewed annually or on the happening of a major economic event, eg. where inflation exceeds wage rises.

awards usually follow. The costs of any agreed increases flow through the economy. If too high, lay-offs can result and businesses may fail.

negligence Occurs when a duty of care has been avoided and a person or property suffers harm or damage. *See* duty of care.

Claims against parties who may have been negligent can be very substantial.

negotiable instrument A security document, the ownership of which passes on delivery to another person free of encumbrance or defect in its title. A simple cheque is negotiable unless the word 'bearer' is struck out.

Securities may be promissory notes, commercial bills or debentures/bonds, or treasury notes payable to bearers.

net The abbreviated term for the Internet. Now in common usage.

net assets (net worth) Total assets less current and non-current liabilities. Shown in the Statement of Financial Position (Balance Sheet).

Net assets are equal to owners' equity. *See also* Statement of Financial Position (Format 2) on p. ix.

net profit/loss Where revenues exceed the cost of goods sold (COGS) and all expenses, the difference is the net profit. Where revenues do not exceed COGS plus expenses, a net loss has occurred.

Recorded on the Statement of Financial Performance (Revenue Statement or Profit & Loss Account).

net profit ratio A profitability ratio calculated as the net profit before tax divided by total sales and expressed as a

It is not unusual for small businesses to be averaging around 1–3% after

N

percentage. When compared to previous years it indicates the trend of the business.

allowing for reasonable living costs.

new economy Used to describe businesses engaged in new technologies, eg. biotechnology, Internet and robotics. Often listed in special stock listings, eg. NASDAQ in the USA. Speculation evident.

New economy businesses tend to have optimistic projections and innovative promotions.

niche market A segment of a total market. *See also* market niche, market segmentation.

no-liability company (NL) An incorporated company whose shareholders are under no liability to pay any unpaid portion of their shares if called up or if the business winds up.

Refers only to a public mining company, which must have the initials NL after its name.

non-current assets Capital assets in a business used for production or revenue-earning rather than as inventory or for exchange. They are depreciable over the economic life of each type.

In the Statement of Financial Position (Balance Sheet). Comprise land, buildings, motor vehicles (not leased), furniture and fittings, plant and equipment.

non-current liabilities Loans due for repayment over a long term. A term loan would be repayable by equal monthly or quarterly instalments. That portion due within the first 12 months would appear as a current liability.

Appear in the Statement of Financial Position (Balance Sheet) where they show the balance of the loan due after allowing for the first 12 months.

non-financial indicators Checks made on aspects of a business that are non-financial, such as customer surveys, quality audits, levels of absenteeism,

The perception of the business in the community is a good test of its relationships.

training program results, staff attitudinal surveys and performance appraisals.

non-profit business An organisation that has been set up to provide a specific service without intending to make a profit.

Charities are an example.

O

obsolescence A loss of value in a product because a newer product may represent better value. Also refers to an asset which is depreciated by use so that it is out of date and no longer economic.

New technologies make older ones obsolescent, eg. computers and cars.

occupational health and safety (OHS) A program adopted by businesses that ensures the conditions in a workplace are safe and consider the welfare of all employees. Required by government legislation. Heavy penalties may apply where a duty of care has not been shown.

State occupational health and safety law (eg. the NSW *Occupational Health and Safety Act* 1983) applies to all business.

old economy The term applied to those listed businesses that have traditionally formed the backbone of a country's economy. In Australia includes BHP, Brambles, Woolworths, Harvey Norman, CSR.

Others are Lend Lease, NAB, Qantas and James Hardie.

on-costs *See* labour on-costs.

on-the-job training Staff training that takes place in the workplace or at the

As distinct from external courses which are meant

desk of an employee. Also known as *in-house training.*

to enhance the abilities of staff.

operating lease The hiring or rental of equipment for a fixed long term (usually over one year) where a monthly tax-deductible payment is made and the contract is cancellable at any time. Does not normally have a residual value, may not allow purchase and is not shown in the body of the Statement of Financial Position (Balance Sheet).

Examples are a fully maintained motor vehicle, rental vehicle, telephone or hire equipment. Disclosure must be made of the amount and the term remaining under the agreement as a note to the Statement of Financial Position (Balance Sheet).

operational plan A component of a business plan leading from the business objectives and its strategy. Seeks to identify specific details for action in the immediate year. Action plans are then prepared for individual tasks.

Include requirements for raw materials to meet production targets, staff and finance needs, inventory levels, etc.

operations management Allocation and maintenance of machinery and resources, eg. raw materials and labour, productivity, quality, wastage and the introduction of new technologies. Operations may refer to a wider sphere of production such as assembly, batch, creative design and packaging. Also referred to as *production management.*

An operations process will require standard costings to which actual cost variations will be compared and actioned. The type of operations in a business may be as varied as the business itself.

option A financial contract that gives the holder the right to buy or sell an asset at a specified price on or before a specified date. Options may be traded for shares and futures.

The holder is not obligated to buy or sell.

ordinary shares Shares issued to owners/ investors in companies that entitle holders to vote and receive dividends or bonus shares. Able to be traded if in a listed public company. *See also* preference share.

When a company ceases operation, ordinary shareholders only receive what is left after all other lenders/ creditors are paid in full.

Organisation for Economic Cooperation and Development (OECD) A 29-member country organisation to which Australia belongs. Acts as a forum for governments to discuss and find solutions to economic, social and other common problems. Statistics are provided quarterly that show unemployment levels, the status of each economy and projections of possible problem issues, eg. environmental.

The Federal Government places much confidence in the independent opinions of the OECD.

organisation structure A diagrammatic presentation of the reporting relationships in an organisation that represent levels of management, authority and accountability at middle to senior levels. Large businesses frequently review this structure and seek to bring greater efficiency through minimising management levels. The type may be pyramidal or flat.

Normally depicts senior relationships but can be extended down to the workplace. As well as the reporting relationship the level on the organisation chart also may depict seniority between others.

organising The structuring of a business and the preparation of all plans ready for implementation and leading towards attainment of the business's objectives. A planning function and a component of the POLC model. This is the 'deciding how to do it' function.

Requires coordination, teamwork, motivation, good communication and generally a good empathy with staff.

outplacement The process of finding a redundant employee other employment.

Outplacement may also involve career transition,

Many larger businesses are now seeking to offer this facility through specialist consultants.

eg. retraining a redundant coal miner for another skill.

outsourcing The contracting to outside firms of certain activities of the business. This may involve accounting or marketing services, staff acquisition, training programs, computer (IT) services, etc. Also called *contracting out*.

Outsourcing may involve agreement for another business to make components for the business. Overseas contractors are often used.

over-award payments Payments made by employers over the minimum award wages.

overdraft A line of credit provided by commercial banks that allows a business to draw in excess of credit funds held. Able to be called in on demand in the event of a breach of the agreed conditions. The security given the bank will normally be a floating debenture charge.

Cheques may be drawn up to the limit of an agreed overdraft for which the business will have provided some security. The facility is a daily working account.

overheads Generally expenses for administration, finance, staff and marketing shown in the Statement of Financial Performance (Revenue Statement or Profit & Loss Account).

Overheads may be fixed costs, such as rent, or variable costs, such as telephones and power.

owners' equity The capital and accumulated funds and reserves shown in the Statement of Financial Position (Balance Sheet) as a liability belonging to the owners or shareholders.

Also known as shareholders' funds or proprietors' funds. *See also* equity.

ownership forms The different ways that businesses operate. Personal liability exists with sole traders or partnerships but is

There may also be tax considerations when choosing which type to operate.

limited where a business incorporates as a proprietary or public company, no-liability company, company limited by guarantee, cooperative or trust company.

P

Pacific rim Refers to those countries that border the Pacific Ocean but also includes India and Sri Lanka which have been included in economic forums under this title. Considered Australia's key market area.

Conferences of Pacific rim countries have been coordinated under the auspices of the Australian Pacific Economic Community (APEC).

paid capital Where a company issues shares for subscription by investors but requests all or a portion only of payment in a call. That proportion not called is known as *uncalled* and is capable of being called at any time. *See also* calls.

par value The value of a share or bond as described in the Constitution (Memorandum of Association). Calculated as the authorised capital divided by the number of shares authorised for issue.

Note the differences between authorised, issued and paid capital.

participation rate The proportion of the population employed or actively seeking employment in the labour market, eg. 68% in 2000.

A measure of economic management in an economy adjusted for seasonality.

participative style The style of management that seeks to include employees in decision-making and elements of management.

partnership A business of no more than 20 partners who enter into an agreement (optional) to operate a business together. Certain professions are allowed over 20 partners, eg. accountants, solicitors (up to 400), veterinarians, architects, chemists (up to 100), doctors and stockbrokers (up to 50).

Distinct from a company. Partners share in any personal liability and an agreement will facilitate dispute handling. Professions may have fidelity insurance.

patent An exclusive right to ownership of an invention, process, machine or form of technology and to assign or sell it for a certain period.

A patent has value and shows under intangible assets in the Statement of Financial Position (Balance Sheet).

payables (trade creditors) *See* accounts payable.

payback period The time taken for the cost of an investment to be recovered by net profit/return. Should allow for an imputed cost for interest. Usually expressed as *x* months or years.

Calculated by how long the accumulated profits take to recover the initial investment.

PAYG (pay as you go) Tax payable to the ATO by quarterly instalments. Based on an ATO-assessed rate applied to the total income of a business. This amount may be underpaid or overpaid when end of year tax returns are calculated.

Payable by all businesses registered for GST and with an ABN. Introduced with the GST in 2000.

PE *See* price earnings.

penalty rates Rates of pay which exceed the normal pay rate per hour. Used for

Changes in workplace conditions are seeing a

excess work hours or out of usual time. Rates may be at time and a half or double time. Also known as *overtime rates*.

reduction in penalty rates due to enterprise bargaining, flexibility and rostering.

people skills Those skills associated with the management of employees through leadership, good communications, interest in employee ambitions, development programs, recognising good results and team-building as well as a good knowledge of the specialist functions of employee relations.

Specialist functions include hiring/firing, industrial relations, training, remuneration policies, etc.

performance appraisal/review The process of assessing the performance of employees against actual results or expectations of the immediate manager.

Identifies the need for further training, advanced training for new roles or specific new tasks ie. in promotion.

perpetual succession The concept of a company having a separate legal existence to its owners and continuing to exist even if ownership changes.

Note that a business or syndicate may be set up for a specific purpose or period.

PERT Abbreviation for Program Evaluation Review Technique. A planning tool (similar to critical path analysis, decision trees and Gantt charts) that presents a sequence of activities and their timing to complete a project. This enables decisions to be made on the costs and resource allocations of concurrent activities.

Used within the construction, manufacturing and engineering industries to facilitate planning and controls.

petty cash A small amount of money (eg. $50–$100) available in an office for buying daily staff needs, eg. milk, sugar, biscuits or stationery items. The total

Very small balances are held in a secure place. Expenses should be properly authorised and

of all receipts is balanced and reimbursed by the business back to petty cash at regular intervals.

petty cash should be balanced back to the initial amount regularly.

piece production Where orders are processed on a piece-by-piece process, eg. a T-shirt made to a unique and specific design and motif, or a one-off, single component production.

Becomes batch production when a selected quantity of the same output is in production.

physical resources Those resources involved in production or distribution, or are non-current assets showing in the Statement of Financial Position (Balance Sheet).

place One of the four major controllable variables in a marketing plan. The place refers to the product being available in the right market to get the best result. Place may be marketplace whereas location may be the site of the business. Factors for choosing both of these are different. *See also* Four P's.

Place will relate to research, target market, domestic or international, channels and costs of distribution.

plaintiff The injured party who brings an action in a civil court.

The *defendant* will contest the claims.

plan *See* business plan.

planned obsolescence The deliberate act of manufacturers to plan components or the product to become unusable or outmoded after a certain period, eg. in computer software.

The replacement of a product by a newer technology differs from the deliberate production of a component that may need replacement after a short period.

planning The 'deciding what to do' stage within the POLC model. Occurs after reviewing the business products, the environment (situational analysis, SWOT, competition), deciding the mission, the objectives and target markets, financial budgets, production plan, marketing plan and expected profitability.

POLC is merely a tool to enable an owner to better manage a business.

planning hierarchy The hierarchy of planning, from the most far-reaching aspects to the most specific, is usually vision → mission → objectives → strategic plan → operational plan including tactical plan → action plans for individuals.

Vision is usually within five years and mission is within 1–2 years. Operational or tactical plans will alter with trade conditions.

POLC model The procedural concept of planning, organising, leading and controlling that is used in the development of business plans, management, communications and decision-making.

politics Term used for a situation in which one person finds minor reasons to denigrate a senior to gain advancement. Not always successful.

Indicates flawed teamwork and an unhappy work environment. To be discouraged.

pollution Contamination of the environment that affects the health and wellbeing of a community. The environment is precious and requires constant protection.

Examples are chemical run-off from farming practices, poor waste disposal, inadequate storage and control practices.

portfolio A listing of investments in shares, contracts or other types of securities that comprises the total holdings of an individual or business.

For example, $10 000 term deposits, 400 CSR shares, 200 treasury notes, property.

P

position description (PD) The presentation of job which comprehensively describes its major attributes, eg. title, who it reports to, location, authorities delegated in the job, major duties, attributes required to carry out the task, remuneration parameters, review procedures, etc. Also known as *job description*.

Position descriptions should be held for all staff. A brief overview of the task and product/service base is often included. The PD is essential before hiring commences and is the basis for all reviews.

positioning Placing products or advertising into a specific market or area for gaining maximum sales.

potential markets Those markets that have not yet been targeted for promotion but which may be entered in the right conditions.

power The ability to direct or influence people. Has various types, eg. reward power of managers to grant rewards, referent power of role models who have desirable characteristics, legitimate power of a senior manager through their delegated authority, coercive power to force others to follow directions (eg. in the military), expert power of people with special and valued knowledge.

There are many cases where power has been unfairly exercised over employees through intimidation. Often these issues are resolved through court action.

precedent The creation and application of a new rule in law.

First established through a court ruling or judgment.

preference share A share issued in a company which pays a fixed dividend each year and also holds a preference for repayment over ordinary shares in the event of a winding up.

Public company listings are tradable.

premium The amount paid over face value for a bond or the excess price paid over valuation for property or another physical asset.

present value The value today of a future payment or stream of payments discounted at the appropriate discount rate. *See also* payback, IRR, DCF.

Used as a method of determining the return on an investment.

prestige pricing Usually a higher price allotted to brands which are well-known and perceived as of higher quality.

For example, BMW and Mercedes cars.

pre-tax profit Net profit before tax has been allowed. Terminology may also include EBIT, earnings before interest and tax.

prevention controls A quality control function that identifies areas within a production line or business that will prevent problems and unnecessary costs. Other controls are concurrent/work-in-progress and feedback. Also known as *feedforward controls*.

Raw material checks, plant maintenance and safety checks are examples. Service and warranty costs are decreased.

prevention costs Expenses incurred to detect variations from acceptable standards for raw materials or components for production.

For example, quality checks and related staff costs.

price One of the Four P's in the marketing mix along with product, promotion and place. Price is the economic value exchanged for consideration. Discounts may reduce revenues.

Price is based on cost of production or cost of acquisition, plus a mark-up to recover expenses and a profit contribution.

P

price discrimination Where a small difference in price can be applied for a minor difference in the product.

price earnings (PE) ratio A profitability ratio applied in a public company where the current share price is divided by the earnings per share (EPS). A good company may have a ratio between 15 and 30. With the hype in new technology stocks, PEs up to 400 are not unknown but the key is EPS or profits. Prices often cannot be sustained in these markets.

In these optimistic high PE markets, investors may take excessive risks, ie. speculating on the stock and future profits increasing.

price skimming Where a business may price new products very highly to establish quick profits until competition or availability pushes prices back to normal

Frequently used for new electronic products, eg. digital TV, DVDs.

primary Refers to industries concerned with agricultural production (eg. agriculture, fishing, forestry) or extraction (eg. gold, coal, bauxite).

primary market Financial market concerned with new share, debenture or bond issues for public companies and governments.

Secondary markets are used for trading.

prime function *See* core business.

prime rate The interest rate at which banks lend money to the most stable or first-class borrowers. Smaller businesses will be charged prime plus a percentage which defines the additional credit risk taken by a lender. Management of the economy can influence the prime rate.

Based on the Reserve Bank of Australia (RBA) rate initially charged for loans to banks. May be influenced by economic indicators.

principal A person who authorises an agent to represent and act on behalf of him/her, eg. a property owner is a principal who uses the services of a real estate agent.

Also, an amount borrowed is known as the principal.

privacy principles Internationally agreed principles covering how data is collected, stored and accessed.

private sector That sector of business activity owned by individuals or private groups and businesses. Also known as *the non-government sector.*

The public sector is the government sector.

private company *See* proprietary company.

privatisation The selling of government or semi-government businesses to the private sector. Done by listing shares on the ASX or by subscription to a prospectus by the public, eg. Qantas, Commonwealth Bank, Telstra, CSL.

This process is usually preceded by a government business commercialising its operation by not receiving any government support.

proactive Taking direct action to control events, rather than waiting until required to act. Control actions should be proactive to avoid problems or added costs.

problem solving The process of carrying out certain procedures to address and solve a business problem satisfactorily. Will involve identifying the problem early and clearly and deciding who should be included in its assessment and whether to involve in-house or external specialist skills. Also involves communicating with employees and obtaining their input,

In addressing various problems, complications may occur which must be clearly identified. At times the best cost-benefit option may not give the best overall results, hence teamwork and possibly identifying options to be taken and, if relevant, completing a cost-benefit analysis to obtain the most suitable expense option.

'brainstorming' may be introduced.

product An item, good or service sold or offered for sale by a business. One of the Four P's vital in developing the marketing mix for all businesses.

Product development involves the idea, research, design, manufacture and packaging of the product.

product differentiation The variation between a number of models of the same basic product, eg. a washing machine with six available models.

product diversification Where a business expands a range of products to spread the risk of one product line declining or to give more market penetration in a brand.

For example, Pacific Dunlop added footwear to tyres.

product knowledge Knowing all about the product, its function, how it operates, its qualities and how it compares with similar brands.

Good salespeople usually have an excellent knowledge of a product and of how to present and finalise a sale.

product liability The accountability of manufacturers and subsequent sellers for the failure of a product to perform as represented. They would usually seek insurance to protect against product liability. The recall of defective products is a means of limiting damages.

The extent of potential liabilities for unsuited or defective products can be measured, especially when referring to medical procedures. Proven claims for damages can be overwhelming.

product life cycle After its creation, a product may find increasing sales, a lag in demand indicating maturity and,

In general terms, products have a life of approximately ten years unless renewed.

unless repackaged or improved, is likely to decline.

product mix The group of products in such proportion as to form a mix that will potentially offer the best profit margins. Not to be confused with the *product range*.

The mix is calculated to give the optimal profit subject to the target market, promotions and costs of distribution.

production management *See* operations management.

productivity The measure of efficiency when comparing the units of input to units of output in a given time. Used as an incentive for reward when measuring output.

The improvement in product output against given benchmarks or standards.

professional indemnity A form of insurance usually taken out by company directors and officers, professional services (eg. doctors, dentists) to protect against financial loss in the event of negligence, mismanagement or fraud.

Company directors must adhere to strict guidelines under the *Corporations Law*. They still may be accountable for mismanagement.

profit Where revenues exceed costs of goods sold plus all expenses, both fixed and variable. *See also* net profit/loss and gross profit/loss.

Profit & Loss Account Now termed the Statement of Financial Performance. Shows the revenues less cost of goods sold (COGS) and expenses of the business to give a net profit or loss for the year. Also referred to as the Revenue Statement in some texts.

This statement for the year will add to owners' equity in the Statement of Financial Position (Balance Sheet) at year end.

P

profit centre A division or area within a business which has both revenues and costs and is expected to generate profits. A business may have a number of profit centres, eg. in a large car company, profit centres might be new sales, second-hand sales, parts and service.

A cost centre does not generate income, eg. administration, employee relations.

profitability The potential to earn or generate profits. The rewards of owners' investments. Profitability ratios can indicate the trend of a business from one year to another or against other similar businesses.

Certain ratios relate net profit to sales and gross profit to sales, funds employed (assets) and owners' equity.

profit sharing The sharing of profits among staff by either bonuses or a range of other benefits, eg. holiday costs, education, housing contributions or entertainment.

Businesses which share profits usually improve their returns and show greater staff loyalty and teamwork.

projections *See* financial forecasts, budgets.

promissory note A note given by a debtor to a creditor promising to pay a certain amount at a given time in the future and usually involves two parties. A *commercial bill* is the term used when the parties are substantial or a bank has added its endorsement as a third party.

A simple promissory note cannot be traded but a commercial bill with businesses of substance and/or bank endorsements can be discounted and traded in money markets until maturity.

promotion One of the Four P's vital to the marketing plan of any business. Involves advertising in all mediums, special sales, discounting, sponsorships, etc.

The task of getting one's products seen, wanted and sold is dependent on the manner and level of promotion.

proprietary company A company incorporated and registered with ASIC as a private company limited to 50 shareholders. It is unable to raise capital from the general public unless with a private placement among friends, when strict rules apply. Requires at least one director and a company secretary. The words 'Pty Limited' must appear in the name.

Share sales and transfer are private and there is little opportunity for selling shares. Shareholder liability is limited to the amount already paid plus any outstanding unpaid share capital in the event of a winding up.

proprietary ratio A profitability/stability ratio where net profit is divided by owners' equity and expressed as a percentage.

See also return on owners' equity (ROE). A good return would be greater than the rate of inflation.

prospectus Required by ASIC when any public company seeks to issue new shares, bonds or debentures to the public. The prospectus must include the latest audited financial statements, forecasts for the business, what the funds will be used for and an investigating accountant's report (normally independent of the auditors).

If statements made in a prospectus are proven incorrect, it can result in action from ASIC or from aggrieved parties

protection The intervention of government to shield against unfair foreign competition or the introduction of disease from foreign organisms. The World Trade Organisation (WTO) may mediate in disputes. Disease control will involve embargos on certain foods.

Certain industries such as footwear, clothing and car manufacture are subject to tariffs, quotas or embargos on imports.

prototype The make-up of a sample product prepared for testing, evaluation, analysis, trial and modification before going into mass production.

Packaging and product may involve a prototype for research., eg. a battery-powered car.

P

provisional liquidator A registered accountant appointed by the court to exercise temporary control over a business which is facing court action from creditors. Usually appointed when a business has concerns about the vulnerability of its assets and applies to the court for a provisional liquidator until the court action begins.

See also winding up, liquidation, receiver.

provisions Refers to special provisions in a business's accounts for potential or known costs which have not yet been incurred.They include liability accounts for annual leave, long service leave and any tax obligations. The costs to increase these provisions each year are treated as a cost to the business showing in the Statement of Financial Performance (Revenue Statement or Profit & Loss Account).

There may also be liability accounts for depreciation of assets and expected bad debts, but these will be shown in the Statement of Financial Position (Balance Sheet) as a deduction against the respective assets.

proxy Where a person is unable to attend personally at a company meeting for voting on an issue and gives authority to another who can vote for them (a *proxy vote*).

Company meetings offer investors the right to appoint nominated persons, eg. a chairperson, to act as proxy.

public company A business which is incorporated or registered as a public company with ASIC to enable it to issue shares and debentures to the public with a prospectus. Also can list on the ASX for trading in its shares or securities. Must have a minimum of 50 shareholders and three directors and place 'Ltd' after its name.

Subject to stringent requirements of the *Corporations Law* and the ASX in maintaining listing for trading.

public liability *See* public risk.

public relations A senior role, usually reporting to the Chief Executive, aimed at creating and maintaining good relations between a business, government entity or charity and its customers and communities. Typically referred to as the 'PR' function in a large entity.

Liaises between the business and the media when public issues or problems arise. Media releases and responses come from the PR executive.

public risk The liability a business has for any of its activities which inflict damage or harm on the members of the public or their property, eg. foreign matter in a food product which causes illness or injury. Also known as *public liability*.

Public liability insurance is usually taken out by businesses to cover potential risk.

public sector That sector of the economy owned and/or controlled by government, semi-government or statutory bodies not otherwise included within the private sector, eg. Telstra, as 49% privatised, is still in the public sector.

Some entities which were once wholly owned by the government were partially privatised at first, eg. Qantas, Commonwealth Bank.

purchase of an established business When considering buying an established business, research should be undertaken, eg. study of the last three years' financial accounts, tax returns, review of the product base, competition, customer base and proprietors' drawings/income.

The use of an independent person (eg. an accountant) even at a cost is better than purchasing a poor business and losing money.

Q

qualities of a leader Ideally a leader should have an entrepreneurial flair, be innovative, have experience in the type of business, be a good people manager and decision-maker, communicate well, have an open door, be proactive and responsive to change and understand financial accounts.

Whilst this is ideal, a good leader will recognise his/her own weakness areas and make use of professional support.

quality assurance (QA) Procedures within a business to improve or maintain all aspects of quality, eg. inspection of all finished goods. An essential element for a business to remain viable.

See also quality circles, total quality management (TQM), quality control.

quality circles Comprise groups of skilled employees gathered together in a process that aims to better the quality of a product/service or procedure that will benefit a customer or the business through decreasing unnecessary costs.

At times quality circles may add costs but these can be justified when the product is improved and more customers purchase it.

quality control Management procedures in place to check the suitability of raw materials, progress of production and product output to minimise reprocessing, seconds, wastage, costs, warranty claims and service problems.

Also may be reflected in the efficiency of the business through receivables collection, inventory controls, etc.

quaternary One of the five groupings of industry types. Comprises information processing, the media, banking, education, real estate and communications businesses.

See also primary, secondary, tertiary, quinary.

quick ratio *See* liquid asset (acid test) ratio on p. xi.

quinary The fifth grouping of industry types comprising the provision of domestic services (both paid and unpaid), entertainment, restaurants and hotel businesses, aged care services and charities and professional services.

Considered the fastest growing sector. *See also* primary, secondary, tertiary, quaternary.

quota Usually a government-imposed restriction placed on the quantity of a product that may be produced or imported into the country. A form of tariff. May be imposed on the production line of a business to avoid overstocking.

Where shares in a new share issue are oversubscribed, a quota may be imposed on the number of shares allocated to certain applicants.

R

random access memory (RAM) Non-permanent memory in a computer's processor which is lost when the power is turned off but which speeds up processing when in use.

rating agency An organisation which provides credit assessments on countries, states, businesses and issued liabilities. A security rating is attached to all issued listed securities or companies. The most secure investments (which usually have the lowest returns) are given a AAA or Aaa rating. The two predominant

A rating of CCC may command a greater return but would be less secure. Agencies carry out extensive research on each country or business before issuing ratings.

rating agencies are Moody's and Standard & Poor's.

ratios *See* p. xi.

ratio analysis The measuring of a business's assets, liabilities or revenue against other groups of assets or expenses to give a meaningful indication of whether a business is improving or deteriorating. Inter-firm comparisons can highlight how one business is performing compared to others in the same industry.

Can be applied to business profitability, efficiency, stability, liquidity areas and include gearing, eg. the current ratio measures liquidity, while the inventory turnover ratio meaures efficiency.

raw materials The components required from suppliers to enable assembly in a production process. The market for raw materials may be both domestic and overseas. Where possible, it is better to add value than to merely supply raw materials.

Australia is said to be well-endowed in its mining, mineral and agricultural resources and provides substantial raw materials to other countries.

reasonable person A term used in legal contexts to describe a person of normal intelligence who is able to perceive surrounding circumstances and who has the knowledge one could expect from a 'normal' person.

For example, it is ideal that jurors in a court case should be 'reasonable' people.

receivables *See* accounts receivable.

receivables (debtors) turnover ratio An efficiency ratio where total credit sales are divided by receivables (preferably averaged for the beginning and end of the year). The result is the number of times receivables turn over in a year. Where a business seeks payment by the end of the

$$\frac{\text{Total credit sales}}{\text{Average receivables}}$$

eg. $\frac{12000}{2000} = 6$ times a year, or every 60 days. Cash flow crises can

following month, which is normal in Australia, 6 times a year (every 60 days) would be considered excellent, but more than 90 days would be a concern.

occur where collections are low and bad debts follow. *See* p. xii.

receiver Usually a chartered accountant appointed by a secured lender (such as a bank) where a borrower has defaulted on a loan. The receiver's task is to control all the assets of the business and collect from available assets any outstanding monies. Once this has occurred the business control returns to the owners unless the creditors instigate provisional liquidation through the courts or the company seeks to be placed under administration. A sole trader may have given property as security, and this would be called in where a default has occurred.

The receiver's duty is only to the bank under an agreement and not to other creditors, although they must be conscious of creditors' claims or any prior charges to the bank. The conduct is legislated by the *Corporations Law* for a company and the *Bankruptcy Act* 1966 for a sole trader or partnership.

recession In economic terms refers to a decline in economic activity. Has been defined in the past as two quarters of negative growth or a reduction in gross domestic product (GDP) per annum since the last quarter. This concept has been dismissed as too restrictive. A recession may reflect in more unemployment, less economic activity, overseas market downturns and exchange rate difficulties.

There are numerous financial indicators and most should be read together to determine whether a recession applies. Economic cycles traditionally move through boom → recession → boom.

recourse Term used in factoring to mean the ability of the factor to recover a debt back from the client. This means the credit risk stays with the client. A factor's pricing will take this into account when

If non-recourse, the factor takes the credit risk and must bear any loss if the debt is not paid.

establishing a service fee (finance costs plus processing and collection costs).

recruitment The process of hiring employees. This will involve analysis of required job skills, preparation of position descriptions, advertising or using recuitment agencies, interviewing, selection, reference-checking, making offers and confirming applications.

Is one of the important functions of the Employment Relations (ER) division. Allied functions of the division include remuneration, induction and training programs.

recycling The reprocessing of discarded materials to transform them into something of more use. Selected domestic garbage and waste are being processed to give garden compost.

Recyclable goods may be paper, plastics, aluminium, glass, etc.

redeemable preference shares Shares issued by a company which take precedence over ordinary shares in the winding up of a company. May be purchased back by the company from investors/holders at some future date. May be traded if listed.

Preference shareholders would receive a return as interest at a fixed rate each year. Ordinary shareholders only receive a dividend when the company declares a dividend, usually from its profits.

redundancy A situation where an employee or group of employees becomes unnecessary because a job no longer exists. Technological change, downsizing, restructuring or simple lack of profitability can cause redundancy. Being made redundant will involve formal notification and a payout.

The Employment Relations division (ER) would handle all personnel issues. Redundancy is one form of downsizing.

re-engineering *See* restructuring

referent power *See* power.

registration Business names and new companies must be registered with ASIC. Similarly, employer organisations, unions, welfare organisations and sector bodies (eg. farmers) need registration to be recognised for input into national wage cases and conciliation tribunals.

There are strict legal requirements to be met to represent sector groups such as the welfare lobby.

regulations When new laws are enacted, they are supported by more detailed procedures. These are known as regulations, which must be followed when related to specific laws.

remuneration Payment for services which is either direct (wages, salaries, directors' fees) or a non-monetary type which can have a monetary value. Remuneration packages can include motor vehicles, health programs, insurance, education costs and overseas travel.

Fringe benefits are subject to tax by the business. The Employee Relations division has responsibility for all remuneration issues.

renewal A stage in the life cycle of a business after establishment, growth and maturity. At this point some businesses may review their product, its packaging and its target market and hence go through a renewal stage.

Other businesses may not renew themselves and could decline towards cessation, bankruptcy or liquidation.

representatives People employed by a business to sell goods or services both for the business and also appointed by other businesses. Promote sales through contact with potential and existing customers.

May also be agents appointed on behalf of a principal such as Ford or Holden.

R

resale price maintenance The process by which a producer fixes the price at which a buyer may resell its product.

The recommended retail price (RRP) is often the means of holding prices at a desirable level within the *Trade Practices Act* 1974.

research and development (R&D) The process of initial research into design, development, packaging and prototypes of a product or service, plus testing before it is offered for sale.

Normally undertaken by a separate department, as development is difficult to control and cost.

reserves Accounts shown separately within owners' equity which are neither capital nor retained earnings. They arise when there has been a revaluation of property to its current value.

Reserves also arise when a premium is obtained where shares in an acquired entity were less than their real value.

resignation The voluntary action taken by an employee to leave an employer. A reason may be to take a position elsewhere.

Letter of resignation normally submitted to the supervisor or manager.

responsibilities to stakeholders The *Corporations Law* recognises that a business's prime purpose is to increase the net worth of its stakeholders. This means its share values increase and/or it pays dividends or issues bonus shares. At times conflicts occur but the prime purpose will remain pre-eminent.

This does not overlook the importance of managing change, social justice, ecological sustainability, compliance with the law and adherence to ethical practices.

resistance to change The main cause of a business opposing change is management which believes in the old methods, is hesitant about the costs of change and is not in touch with developments in the

The concept of 'dynamic conservatism', whereby owners and staff are happy with things as they are, leads to owners putting off

market or in technology. Employees often do not like or want change and are concerned about disruptions, downsizing and taking on new tasks. The culture of a business may not be receptive unless a change charter is incorporated into staff induction and training.

needed improvements. Different stakeholders may have different reasons for resisting change.

restrictive covenants Conditions inserted into an agreement to restrain certain activities. Examples typically involve people who have acquired certain intellectual property from a previous employer not being able to set up in business within a certain geographic area, or purchasing a block of land with certain restrictions as to what may be built on it.

Under the *Trade Practices Act* 1974 certain restrictions placed on a person's right to earn a living may be illegal. In most cases legal opinions would be sought to ensure compliance with the Act.

restructuring The review and implementation of new reporting and communication relationships that is intended to improve the efficiency of an organisation. *Disintermediation* refers to the process of minimising processes and cutting out middle levels of management as well as the sales levels between manufacturer and customer.

Often results in a new organisation structure with more senior managers reporting to the Chief Executive. Restructuring results in downsizing, staff movement and cost savings.

retailing The practice of selling, including shops selling to customers, direct selling through the Internet, television and e-commerce, and door-to-door selling. Some traditional shop-selling may be under threat as advancing technology changes the nature of the retail industry.

The move towards cutting out service levels between manufacturers and customers, known as *disintermediation*, will impinge upon retailing in the future.

retained earnings/profits Profits retained in the business and not otherwise paid out to owners as dividends. They add to the owner's equity in a business as a source of funds on the Statement of Financial Position (Balance Sheet). They are an accumulation of earnings shown each year in the Statement of Financial Performance (Revenue Statement or Profit & Loss Account).

Retained or accumulated profits may be used to pay dividends in the future. Retained earnings add equity and improve gearing ratios, and retained cash will improve working capital.

retirement The voluntary action of an employee who leaves the workforce permanently after years of service.

Usually (but not necessarily) occurs when men reach 65 years and women a slightly lesser age.

retraining The process of training existing employees who are being redeployed into another role, promoted or developed to add more skills for greater value to a business.

A need for retraining is often identified in a performance appraisal. The Employment Relations department controls this.

retrieval Accessing information that has been stored in computer programs or on disk. Businesses are now electronically storing most hard copy data to meet tax obligations.

Certain original data must still be retained for legal reasons.

return on assets A measure of profitability in a business where net profit is divided by the total assets in a business and then expressed as a percentage.

Ideally the return should be greater than the rate of inflation.

return on capital A ratio sometimes used where there are no accumulated profits or reserves. Usually in this case

The inclusion of the total owners' investment, including retained earnings

the ratio which is used is the return on owners' equity (shareholders' funds) ratio (see below).

and any reserves, is the meaningful measure.

return on investment (ROI) A ratio used to calculate the profit return on a specific investment. It is expressed as a percentage of net profit arising from the investment divided by the cost of the investment. This is distinct from return on owners' equity, often referred to as ROE.

This measure, while useful, does not take account of time or the cashflow effect of payment streams. These may include payback, IRR and DCF analysis.

return on owners' equity (shareholders' funds) A profitability ratio. Calculated by dividing net profit after tax by owners' equity in a company (or the accumulated capital in any other business) expressed as a percentage. The return on assets will differ between industry types. It is not uncommon for a small business generally to return slightly more than the inflation rate.

Where a company has preference shares the dividend is deducted from the profit. If there are intangible assets they should be deducted from owners' equity before doing the calculation.

revenue Income from sales of goods or services relating to a business. Shown as Income on the Statement of Financial Performance (Revenue Statement or Profit & Loss Account).

Receipts from the sale of assets, interest and dividends received from investments, or rent from assets used by others is classed as Other Income.

Revenue Statement *See* Statement of Financial Performance (which is the accepted term for Revenue Statement or Profit & Loss Account).

Standards are set by the Australian Accounting and Public Sector Standards Boards.

reverse discrimination Where anti-discrimination policies are applied

For example, where women are given equal opportunity

properly but advantage is taken to apply a reverse policy.

to attain senior roles but once in the roles prefer to appoint other women.

reward power *See* power.

rights issue An issue of ordinary shares to existing shareholders where each shareholder receives the right to an additional number of ordinary shares in proportion to their current holding.

These may be issued and traded where a company's shares are listed.

risk **(1)** Where related to investment, refers to the chance of loss when investing in a project with a high rate of return. For example, investment in a project offering a return of 50% a year would be risky. A return over 20% would warrant care. **(2)** Where related to a business venture there are industry risks, eg. coal mines closing, special risks such as flooding or fire, diversification risks where one product has not been given due attention, government risks or systematic risks, eg. an ATO/legal decision which can affect all businesses in certain schemes.

Lenders face a number of financial risks. For example, *default risk* of non-payment, *interest rate risk* of the variable rate increasing to an unsustainable level, *liquidity risk* of a business not being able to make monthly payments, *security risk* where the security deteriorates or *documentary risks* where the agreement is legally defective.

risk management Steps taken to protect a business from any eventuality which may adversely affect its viability. A business which trades in money markets or borrows in overseas currencies must take certain protective measures to minimise the risk of loss. This function falls within the role of a Financial Controller.

Insurance policies may be taken for certain specified risks eg. burglary, fire, loss of profits, machine breakdown, fraud or embezzlement, public liability, etc. Use of forward cover and of hedging is normal in financial transactions.

robotics The use of computer software that enables machinery to perform mechanical tasks through robots, replacing people on an assembly line. Car assembly is one example.

The term is also used when referring to the science of designing and building robots.

S

safety net The minimum requirements set out in awards for various industries as legislated by government and maintained by the AIRC. Managed by the Employee Relations division in large companies.

The safety net comprises fair and enforceable minimum wages and conditions of employment not otherwise covered by enterprise agreements.

sale and leaseback The practice of selling assets (eg. property, motor vehicles, plant and equipment) to raise capital and then leasing them back for use by the business. This may occur where business growth has reduced the working capital so that the business is restricted from trading efficiently or even obtaining credit from suppliers. Cash from the sales is introduced, thus improving working capital.

Lease costs are all deductible for tax purposes. The sale of property can potentially offer cash well in excess of the historical cost reflected in the accounts.

sales analysis The listing of each product sold by number, value and margin for comparison against budgets, and individual performance targets of wholesalers, distributors or sales personnel.

Often presented to management monthly for decision-making and remedy where necessary.

sales mix The combination of product sales made in a period. In reality, the budgeted sales mix may not always be achieved.

samples Products distributed to prospective customers free of charge to promote future sales.

sanctions **(1)** Approval by agreement as to what is right and what is wrong. **(2)** Measures taken by one or more countries to restrict or prohibit trade or contact with another country which has broken international law.

May arise from an industrial dispute where employees may place sanctions on another business's goods.

scabs The term often used to describe non-union workers who do the work of unionists during a strike or dispute.

Now that membership of a union is voluntary this term has less meaning.

scheduling The planning for supplies of various materials or labour needed for a project so that they are ready at the right time and place.

See also critical path analysis, PERT and decision trees as other methods of planning projects.

scientific management *See* classical/scientific management.

scrip Stock or share certificates indicating ownership of shares in a company and entitling the holder to vote at meetings, sell the shares or obtain dividends.

Scrip is increasingly being used to describe an increasing range of securities eg. debentures, asset-backed securities (ABS).

secondary markets Capital markets in which existing securities may be traded. These will involve stockbrokers,

Primary markets are where new shares, debentures or treasury

investment banks, money market operators, commercial banks, corporations, individuals and often the ASX and the Sydney Futures Exchange (SFE).

notes are first issued.

secondment The temporary transfer of an empioyee to another business for a period so that he/she may carry out a specific task, learn new skills or gain exposure to a different environment.

Correspondent relationships with overseas businesses often allow secondment for training.

secret ballot The casting of a vote that is confidential (as in State and Federal elections). Secret ballots are frequently requested at company or other meetings where voters have the right to request that a vote be anonymous.

There are occasions when it is not in the best interests of voters to disclose their intentions. Secret ballots are necessary in union appointments.

secured creditors Usually banks or other entities owed money which hold a formal charge over either specific assets or, in the case of a company, a floating charge which secures all the assets of the business. Loans may have been given only when security was available. *See also* unsecured creditors.

A secured creditor may call in a loan where a default has occurred. In the event of a business failure a secured creditor will have preference over unsecured creditors.

securities Various types of financial instruments offered by government or companies to investors. Such securities may be traded if the borrower is a listed public company. The underlying assets of government or of a business are pledged as security for such financial instruments. *See also* financial instruments.

They include shares, debentures, government bonds or notes, unit trust certificates or rights to money that has been lent or deposited.

security The charge given over an asset or assets which will be given over to a lender if the borrower defaults on a loan.

Company charges are recorded with the Australian Securities and Investment Commission (ASIC).

seed capital *See* venture capital.

selling and distribution expenses Costs incurred in selling a product or service. There are four major expense categories: administration, finance, staff and marketing. Selling and distribution expenses are components of marketing expenses.

Includes advertising and promotion, displays, distribution costs such as freight and couriers, commissions, sales bonuses, discounts and sales, car expenses.

semi-government securities Stocks issued by a State Government utility, such as an electricity authority or water board, offering a rate of return generally at a margin above that for a Commonwealth bond.

senior management Employees at the highest level of management, usually comprising the Chief Executive and all directly reporting subordinates.

sensitivity analysis Analysis which involves altering individual costs to compare the expected profits. Used in feasibility studies and relates to the 'what if' questions, eg. assessing expected profits of a project if one cost is higher or lower.

To obtain the best results, cost analyses usually involve a number of separate cost variables.

severance pay The payment made when an employee is retrenched. States have differing rates for various terms of employment.

In NSW, over four years' service provides a pay entitlement of eight weeks' pay.

share buyback Where a business which is listed seeks to repurchase the shares of existing shareholders, rather than seek out another investment. The buyback of a company's own shares is done for two major reasons: to allow consolidation of its existing core business, and to reduce the share capital to improve the earnings per share on a lesser number.

There are also times when a public company may seek to target its core business activities by selling off some divisions, eg. Burns Philp sold BBC Hardware and NRMA floated its insurance subsidiary.

shares A company will issue a certificate of ownership to investors in the equity in a business for the number of shares they each hold. May refer to ordinary or preference shares issued by a business. Shares may be authorised, issued, called and paid up or partly paid.

Shares are also known as *stocks*, which is more commonly used in the United States.

shareholder A person or institution that holds shares in a company. Shareholders have the right to vote, obtain dividends or bonus shares and to sell their shares or any rights to shares that may be issued.

Known as *stockholders* in the USA.

short-term borrowing Borrowing for a period of (usually) less than one year for a specific purpose. Such borrowing would show in the Statement of Financial Position (Balance Sheet) as a current liability.

An example may be the purchase of equipment with repayment made over 6 months, or a temporary cash requirement pending a permanent loan.

situational analysis An assessment of a business's current position, eg. its product's market share, increase or decrease in profitability, competition, the direction of the economy, external and internal influences on the product, etc. A

Research and a review of the financial accounts pertaining to a product will be crucial to undertaking a situational analysis.

S

situational analysis is a component of a marketing plan usually followed by a more detailed SWOT analysis that will assist in determining marketing objectives and strategies.

skills analysis Undertaken by Employment Relations departments to identify the level and qualifications of all staff in a business in order to highlight potential training needs. *See also* job analysis.

small business A business that is independently owned and operated in which management makes all the decisions, or one which has a relatively small share of the market in which it operates. The Australian Bureau of Statistics (ABS) defines small business as one which has less than 20 employees in a non-manufacturing business, or has less than 100 employees in a manufacturing business.

Small business is the major employer (58%) of labour in Australia where over 900 000 businesses may meet these definitions (ABS, 2000).
The *Corporations Law* defines 'small' as less than 50 employees, turnover under $10 m and assets under $5 m.

small/medium enterprises (SMEs) A term often used when referring to small businesses as described above.

social contract An agreement between major social organisations and governments about major economic, social or environmental issues. Such an organisation may be the Australian Council for the Coordination of Social Services (ACCOSS) or The Heritage Trust.

Include protection of the environment, wildlife, heritage, welfare or the disadvantaged.

social justice A general concept of fairness and responsibility in society. In

A business has its prime responsibility in law to its

business, refers to a business's responsibility to its customers, its community, the society in which it operates, the environment and to ideals which the community believes in.

shareholders or owners, but closing an unprofitable branch (eg. of a bank) may not meet the social justice aims of a community

social responsibility The perception, increasing in many communities, that business must have more concern for what it does in its communities. This refers to environment, commitment to education, training, sporting activities and also to ensuring minimum services.

Banks have been closing branches in rural and many urban centres and there has been a backlash against this. New methods of servicing customers are emerging.

social wage The total wage plus other benefits received from a business and/or government into a household, eg. family benefits for families and tax deductions for non-working spouses.

Often dictated by minimum awards and the government safety net.

sole trader A person who owns and is solely responsible for a business. A business name is required to be registered with ASIC unless the name is the same as the owner.

A sole trader will have unlimited personal liability for all debts, while a company has limited liability.

solvency The state in which a business is capable of paying all its debts as they arise or fall due. A company which continues to trade when it is unable to pay its debts can impose a personal liability on its directors.

The current and liquid asset (quick asset) ratios are intended to identify the solvency or liquidity in the business (an insolvent business will lack liquidity).

sources of finance The lenders and institutions that will loan money to people or businesses, usually for specific purposes against suitable security. Some

Sources of business finance are banks, investment banks, building societies, credit unions,

businesses will buy business assets and lease them back to the previous owner, eg. property, motor vehicles, plant & equipment. Not to be confused with *types* of finance. *See* p. xvii for more details.

finance leasing and factoring companies.

span of control In a business organisation structure, the span of control refers to the number of people who come directly under the control of another.

The larger the business, the greater the span of control may be. A Chief Executive may have up to 12 managers reporting.

specific performance An order by a court to a party in breach of an agreement to fulfill the terms of the agreement. For example, if a builder was not paid progress payments as agreed, a court could order the defaulting party to perform what was originally agreed upon.

speculator A person who takes a position in a market simply to make a profit and who has no interest in the commodity traded. May be in shares, bonds or derivatives/commodities.

Often people who are prepared to risk money with little research.

spot In foreign exchange transactions, this means cash settlement within two working days.

spot rate/price The price applying now for immediate delivery.

staff authority The authority given to support service managers such as Employment Relations or the Financial Controller to take certain decisions or give directions to line managers and/or their subordinates.

staffing The process of employing staff to required positions in a business. This will include a position requirement, preparation of a position (job) description, hiring from advertisements, using consultants, reallocating internally, reviewing resumes, interviews, selection, checking references, making an offer and receiving an acceptance.

One of the duties of an Employment Relations Manager (HRM). Staffing needs often arise from the annual business plan, which will include a staffing (personnel) plan.

stakeholders Those people having an interest in a business in some way. They may be internal, such as employees and owners, or external, such as shareholders, customers, suppliers, lenders, the local community or society in general. Sporting teams may be stakeholders through corporate sponsorships.

While people generally may have no apparent direct investment in a business they become stakeholders where a business plays a part in a community.

Statement of Cash Flows A summary of the cash flows inwards (receipts) and outwards (payments) in a small business, normally shown under three headings in public company reporting, eg. operating, investing and financing activities. This statement is one of the three major reports required in an Annual Report, along with a Statement of Financial Position (Balance Sheet) and Statement of Financial Performance (Revenue Statement or Profit & Loss Account).

Cash control in a business should be a daily task. Cash flow forecasts predict the movement of cash in and out and compare this to to available cash facilities.

Statement of Financial Position Current term for what was previously known as the Balance Sheet. The financial statement of a business that shows the amounts owned and the amounts owed, including to owners in a business, at a point in time.

Assets owned
eg. inventories
Liabilities owed
eg. loans

Equity = owners' funds
Assets = liabilities + owners' equity

Statement of Financial Performance Current term for what was previously known as either the Profit & Loss Account or the Revenue Statement. Shows the revenues less cost of goods sold (COGS) and expenses of the business to give a net profit or loss for the year.

This statement for the year will add to retained earnings/profits in owners' equity in the Statement of Financial Position (Balance Sheet) at year-end.

statutes Written laws made and enacted by government.

statutory enterprises Certain businesses which are carried out under specific statutes. Usually government or semi-government enterprises businesses, eg. the ABC as governed by the *Australian Broadcasting Corporation Act* 1983.

Many utilities in electricity water, waste disposal, etc, are statutory enterprises. Lately some have been privatised.

Statutory Reserve Deposits (SRDs) Funds required by the Reserve Bank of Australia to be deposited by trading banks as a means of regulating levels of credit in the community.

These SRDs may change according to Reserve Bank policies in assisting management of the economy with governmen

stocks *See* inventories. Also a general word (used in the US) for shares, debentures and bonds.

stock control *See* inventory control.

stocktake Systematic counting of all inventory held by a business. Essential for effective inventory/stock control.

Usually carried out half-yearly to prove the correctness of computer records and to give confidence in reporting.

stockturn *See* inventory turnover ratio.

strategic alliances Where two or more countries, businesses or political parties join together for a common aim, such as addressing a threat, taking up an opportunity or developing an important idea.

The formation of the European Union (EU) was seen as a strategic alliance of countries. The merger of BHP with Billiton was a strategic alliance.

strategic planning The planning of the course of action for a business for a term of up to five years. Sets out the procedures required to meet the business objectives. Due to the action of competitors, strategies may change over time. Based on the business plan where the objectives of the business are determined.

The annual operational plan comes from the strategic plan and sets out the procedures to be undertaken in the immediate year towards meeting the business objectives.

strategy A plan to achieve a given result or advantage in meeting a business's objectives, mission or vision.

strike A refusal to do something, eg. employees may refuse to work to seek higher wages or better conditions, or to avoid retrenchment.

Often requires negotiation, mediation or some form of compromise suitable to all parties.

structural change *See* restructuring.

structural efficiency principle (SEP) A set of guidelines that aims to make Australian business better able to compete globally.

The increase in enterprise bargaining, employee profit participation, promotion of

This means management restructuring, improved employee/employer relations that offer better career path planning, staff development, multiskilling, employee participation in decision-making and an emphasis on productivity and flexibility. Globalisation is requiring more teamwork.

change through change charters and acceptance of new ideas that enhance business results or allow a competitive advantage will all improve structural efficiency.

subsidy Financial assistance given by a government to assist businesses to compete effectively. This may involve assistance to develop a new process or invention.

Governments may also provide tariff and quota limits to assist certain businesses, eg. car manufacture.

subsidiary company A company which is wholly owned by another company (known as the parent or holding company). It is still deemed a subsidiary if the parent holds 20% or more of the shares.

Subsidiaries where another company owns over 20% of its capital are known as *controlled entities*.

sugging Obtaining access to a customer in a certain manner, eg. gaining entrance to a home and then intending to sell a related product.

Some door-to-door salespeople use this method to gain entry and then seek to sell a product, eg. a vacuum cleaner.

summary dismissal Where an employee is dismissed without notice. Usually occurs where there has been theft, misappropriation of monies, fraud, embezzlement or some other form of misconduct, eg. drunkenness or insubordination.

Dismissal of an employee normally requires certain procedures, eg. written advice, training and counselling.

summons An instruction given by a court to a defendant to either pay a plaintiff or attend the court for hearing of a claim.

Issued as a first step in a legal action when all other negotiation has failed.

superannuation The money invested for employees which is able to be withdrawn after a certain age for retirement or other valid purpose. Payments are required to be made by employers under government legislation to approved superannuation funds on behalf of employees.

Government required that employers pay employee superannuation from 1992.

supply chain Refers to the movement of raw materials, goods or services from one stage to the next. For example, from a primary industry or initial supplier to another for adding value, then through distribution to retailers and ultimately to customers.

A well-structured economy has sound and stable supply chains. An emerging economy tends to have a disjointed and uncertain supply chain.

support services Parts of a business which are not always directly engaged in its prime function but which are essential to achieve its purpose. These include internal finance and administration, marketing, information technology (IT), employment relations, research and development and public relations. Other external network services may include membership of an industry group, a Chamber of Commerce, local sports clubs or schools.

The extent to which these support functions have been set up is dependent on the size and complexity of the business. Large businesses place great emphasis on their formal and informal networks. Care must be taken to avoid aspects of collusion., eg. price fixing which is illegal under the *Trade Practices Act* 1974.

survey A questionnaire used in business to find out people's opinions and behaviour. Assists a business in determining its product positioning in the business plan.

sustainable competitive advantage An advantage a business holds which will

May involve the rights to a process (Microsoft®

S

maintain its competitiveness and can be sustained through unique ownership.

Windows) or even ownership of a water spring in a rural area.

SWOT analysis The listing of the internal strengths and weaknesses and external opportunities and threats affecting a business. Important tool for a business to determine how best to meets its objectives for the year.

Usually follows a situational analysis or general overview of the business environment. A vital step in the planning process.

Sydney Futures Exchange (SFE) Commenced in 1960 and now offers trading in commodity futures, financial futures such as interest rates, financial indices, bank bills, options etc. While this market may offer improved risk management, it can be highly speculative.

Related to the ASX and also to other international futures exchanges, eg. Chicago. Members who trade must be suitably qualified.

syndication The joining together of a group of people or businesses to carry out a project together with a common objective.

It may be for profit, for sharing costs, for mutual recognition, etc.

system A way of organising, programming and working efficiently to a fixed plan or set of rules to achieve a desired result.

systematic risk That part of a security's risk that cannot be eliminated by diversification, but which can be affected by ATO or legal definitions or changes.

See also risk.

systems analyst A specialist whose task is to define, identify and analyse business problems for solutions using various computer programs. The outcomes should improve efficiency, methods, planning and controls.

These people will be proficient in the programs used by a business and capable of drawing on new technologies.

systems management The management of the Information Technology (IT) division of a business and the systems hardware and software on which it operates. This area is becoming more complex as issues of communication, data collection, reporting, analysis and new technologies have impacts on business.

The vast progress in communications through satellites, technology through computers and opportunities through the Internet will both enhance business and cause problems with managing such progress.

T

tactical planning Also known as operational planning but more short-term and capable of being changed at short notice to meet competitive issues. For example, the operational plan should apply for one year but a tactical amendment may need to be made within it at some stage.

The hierarchy of planning is normally the vision, mission, objectives, strategic plan, operational plan (including tactical plan) and action plans for individuals

takeover Usually the forcible taking over of one business by another by offering to buy shares in the company being purchased at a certain price. Such an action with public companies requires a formal offer document being presented to all shareholders of the company being purchased. *See also* merger.

Assumes that one company is seeking to forcibly absorb another within its culture. Where a takeover has mutual agreement from both businesses the term *merger* is preferred.

tangible assets Assets that are clear, definite or physical. Comprise trading and capital items showing in the Statement of

Includes items such as cash, inventories, investments, plant,

Financial Position (Balance Sheet), and distinct from intangible assets such as trademarks, logos, patents, etc.

furniture, motor vehicles, property, fittings and equipment.

target market The group or specific groups of customers or a geographic area chosen by the business where it intends to promote its products, eg. small businesses tend to target customers in their immediate vicinity.

Research will have been undertaken to assist a business in defining its target market.

tariff A government tax imposed on imported goods, usually to curtail dumping by other countries of cheap products or to give a measure of protection to a domestic industry.

For example, Australian motor vehicle manufacturers have a measure of protection through government tariffs.

taxation Income received by governments from individuals and businesses based on various rates. Income taxes are applied at progressive rates for individuals; company tax is paid based on the rate at the time.

Compulsory taxes apply against net profits and include GST, excise, transaction taxes, PAYG and withholding tax.

tax haven A country (usually small) where registered businesses pay low taxes or none at all. Many companies have endeavoured to minimise their tax liabilities by using such countries for registering their businesses. Australia has a blanket condition that any action taken with the prime intention to avoid standard taxation may be held to be illegal.

Countries which have offered such facilities are the Cook Islands, Cayman Islands and the Netherlands Antilles to name a few.

tax minimisation Every individual and business is entitled to minimise their taxation liabilities by structuring their businesses in such a way that deductions are maximised. It is illegal, however, to

Ultimately the ATO or the courts make determinations on disputed taxation claims.

make any arrangement that is intended to avoid tax.

t-commerce The process of carrying out business transactions utilising the television. Requires remote control for accessing various services, eg. shopping, gaming, investments, news, opinions, email communications, etc. This term is increasingly being used when referring to e-commerce transactions.

The prefix 'e-' is used for electronic services in many emerging areas eg. email, e-commerce, e-business, etc.

teamwork The ability of individuals to bring their specific strengths into a group and work together effectively. The aim is to encourage enhanced performance, trust, loyalty, commitment and equity.

technology The combination of knowledge, machinery and innovative ideas to transform resources into more useful products.

Technology is vital in today's global business environment.

telemarketing Use of the telephone to promote products or services.

Extending also to interactive television services.

telementoring Use of tutoring through the medium of either telephone or television and using the technologies of the Internet.

An emerging area for education, training and head-to-head tutoring for various courses and skills.

tendering The process of lodging a quotation for supply of goods and services to an organisation which has advertised for quotations.

Tenders are then assessed and the successful tenderer is awarded the contract.

terminal Also known as a computer remote terminal (CRT) or visual display unit (VDU), the hardware monitor including keyboard, mouse and visual aid (camera) for sending and receiving data from a base computer.

term loan A bank loan of a fixed amount drawn down in full or by separate draw-downs repayable over a specified period by equal monthly or quarterly instalments. Often used to acquire capital equipment or to improve the liquidity or working capital of a business. Investment banks, finance companies, credit unions and building societies may also make term loans with suitable security being offered.

A term loan payable within 12 months is treated as a current liability and the portion due over 12 months as a non-current liability in the Statement of Financial Position (Balance Sheet).

terms of trade The relationship between countries based on the total value of goods and services purchased or sold between them. Compares the prices received for exported goods or services and the prices paid for imports.

Used by economists to identify the volume of trade between countries and to project likely influences. Assists exporters to seek out target markets.

tertiary That sector of the economy related to service functions and including all retailing, building construction, transport and communications.

Includes education and training institutions, among other things.

time payment *See* hire-purchase.

times interest earned (interest cover) ratio A measure of the number of times net profit (EBIT) covers the interest costs in a business. This is a stability ratio as a low cover can indicate heavy borrowing or the use of expensive credit.

$$\frac{\text{Profit/earnings before interest and tax}}{\text{Total interest costs}}$$

A cover of less than three times may concern bankers.

tort A civil (as opposed to criminal) wrong done to another person and likely to be actioned in court.

total quality management (TQM) A concept in business where all employees are involved in programs to achieve optimum standards of quality throughout all aspects of a business. The 'father' of this concept was an American, Edward Deming, who first involved Japan in the process. This concept is being extended to incorporate change policies in a business.

Recognises the value of quality in minimising wastage, getting repeat business, public perception and improved profits. Globalisation has now forced change policies to be added to TQM as a desirable objective.

trade agreements Where two or more businesses or countries agree on a set of written principles in relation to any mutual trading matter between them with the intention of improving the efficiency of a market or trade.

The Closer Economic Relations (CER) agreement is intended to facilitate trade between Australia and New Zealand.

trade associations Usually established by employer groups within specific industries for the purpose of better liaising with governments, unions and social/environmental groups to further their mutual interests.

Under trade practices legislation however collusion in price fixing is illegal., eg. with oil/petrol, construction tendering, etc.

trade credit The credit allowed to purchasers buying goods/services. Usually extends to 30 days, which in Australia means a purchase in one month is due for payment by the end of the following month. Discounts can be offered for early payment.

Businesses that offer credit to customers must have clearly defined credit and collection policies. If they do not, bad debts can occur.

trademark A logo, name or symbol registered to give exclusive use only to the registered party or their franchisee. They are important in promoting brands to the market, customers, suppliers and others.

Examples are Adidas, Microsoft® Windows and Nike names and logos.

trade practices legislation Federal legislation that bans price-fixing, industry collusion, antisocial behaviour, unethical business practices such as pyramid selling and false advertising. Also regulates the sale of dangerous goods, eg. guns, certain chemicals, sprays, etc. First established as the *Trade Practices Act* 1974.

Legislation is administered by the Australian Competition and Consumer Commission (ACCC) in conjunction with ASIC.

trade unions Associations of employees in specific industry groups. They may act for employees with employers, governments or other trade unions to improve wages, conditions of employment, health and safety, education and other related issues. Unions are amalgamating and their power over the last few years has reduced. Unions may be craft, industrial, occupational or miscellaneous.

Historically, trade unions required mandatory employee membership. Now it is voluntary. Negotiations may include unions in enterprise bargaining or award negotiations, eg. Australian Workers Union, Teachers Federation, Transport Workers Union.

trading account A calculation for identifying gross profits. Shows sales less cost of goods sold (COGS) broken down by their component parts, eg. opening inventory plus purchases or production, freight, direct costs of production including wages, less closing inventories. The resulting gross profit is transferred to the Statement of Financial Performance (Revenue Statement or Profit & Loss Account). Manufacturing organisations may use this account.

Use of this account is much less common today since all items are now included in the Statement of Financial Performance (Revenue Statement or Profit & Loss Account).

trainee A person employed early in his/her career and given special training,

Advancement will always be greater with a

irstly through business induction then in pecialist tasks or through an pprenticeship. They are trainees until ufficiently advanced in experience, age nd/or position.

core knowledge and understanding of business basics.

training The preparation of employees to indertake existing or new tasks proficiently. Training and development of staff is vital for maximising employee value, achieving ambitions, promotions, encouraging innovation and improving eamwork and loyalty.

Training may be internal or involve external courses. New technologies have stressed the importance of this function within Employment Relations.

training and development A movement within employee training which emphasises more general development programs that will enhance the abilities and value of employees.

A business that does not show an interest in employee ambitions may have a higher staff turnover.

training needs analysis This is undertaken by the Employment Relations division of larger companies and involves an analysis of the skills held by employees in all positions and of the skills required to meet objectives or change. It identifies the need for both internal and external courses of improvement.

The major issues in training are multiskilling, rostering, scheduling of staff, changes in communications and the Internet.

transfer The act of moving an employee from one position to another by location, task or through promotion.

Such transfer may be geographic, positional or departmental.

transfer of title When ownership of an asset is transferred onto a buyer or where property is legally noted on a title as being owned by another.

Conveyancing is the process of settling and transferring property transactions for buyers and sellers.

T

transfer pricing The prices at which services, goods, property both tangible and intangible, are traded across international borders between related parties. There are a number of methods of calculating transfer prices, some of which require ATO approval.

The Organisation for Economic Cooperation and Development (OECD) guidelines have been established to assist in calculating the method of pricing.

transnational (multinational) corporation A business which operates both inside and outside its own country's boundaries. Usually they are large, multiproduct/service enterprises with interests in a range of diversified products, eg. BHP/Billiton with interests in mining, oil, aluminium, diamonds, gas, etc. News Corporation, Brambles and Campbells Soups/Arnotts are others.

These businesses are also major drivers of globalisation, innovation and new technologies (such as communications). Their role can substantially enhance lesser-developed economies as well as increase competition for Australian business.

trust deed A document which appoints a separate trustee company to a business that issues securities. The trustee will oversee the conduct of the business and all aspects relating to the securities, and the trust deed sets out the terms of issue and certain undertakings by the business.

Trustee companies such as Permanent Trustee, Public Trustee and others offer their services.

trustsBusiness entities which own assets on behalf of nominated beneficiaries and where profits may be distributed according to the rules of the trust. Trusts are often managed by a company or financial institution and the trust may issue units to members which may be traded, based on the value of units, from time to time.

Family trusts are sometimes set up to pay educational or other future costs and to give a tax benefit for children, or to protect their right to capital sums which may have been left to them by others.

turnover The term used when referring to total sales of a business or revenues. *See* revenue.

types of finance There are four major categories of finace: equity, debt, factoring and leasing. *Equity* is invested as capital or in the shares of a company by investors/owners and venture capital companies, and also comes from earnings of the business. *Debt* is borrowed by a business. It requires payment of an interest charge and some form of security for the lender. The amount of debt in a business will depend on size, ability to pay interest, profitability and management expertise. *See also* factoring, leasing.

Types of debt will include overdrafts, term loans, commercial bills, hire-purchase, debentures trade credit, receivable loans, personal loans and mortgages (usually over property). *Leasing* may be the rental of equipment or where sale and leaseback has occurred. *Factoring* is the sale of receivables and provides finance as sales invoices are raised.

U

ultra vires Means 'outside the purpose' (Latin) and is a term used when a business carries on an activity which is outside its stated purpose as set out in its Constitution.

Sometimes a business may have done something outside the owners' purpose; if so, it may be held by the court to be illegal or unauthorised.

un-Australian The term used to refer to an action that is not in keeping with the (perceived) culture, beliefs, ethics or philosophies of Australian society. The arbitrary charging of certain costs by

For example, taking advantage of a disadvantaged person would be 'un-Australian' or even illegal.

some banks may be construed by some as un-Australian. Aspects of social justice and equity may be included.

undercapitalisation The situation where a business starts with insufficient funds or where it expands with inadequate planning for funding its new level of business. A major cause of business failure.

Evidenced by very low current and liquid asset ratios, low or no working capital, minimal bank facilities and constraints on trading in the business.

underwriter When a business issues a prospectus for new shares or debentures, certain businesses may offer to 'underwrite' the issue which means they agree to buy any unsubscribed shares or debentures not otherwise taken up by the public.

Underwriters are usually stockbrokers, some major public companies, institutional investors or investment banks. The shortfall taken up may be sold on the market in the future.

unfair dismissal The sacking of an employee without following standard dismissal procedures. Employees must obey lawful and reasonable commands, use care and skill and act in good faith and may be dismissed if these conditions are not met. However, if unfair dismissal occurs, an employer may face a claim through the Australian Industrial Relations Commission (AIRC) Tribunal or court.

Dismissal may be unfair if written advice has not been made on three occasions, opportunity has not been given for the employee to improve, or the correct severance procedures were not followed.

unfranked dividends The dividends paid by a company which have not had any tax paid on them, thus making them taxable in the hands of an investor. *See also* franked dividends.

unincorporated business A sole trader or partnership in which the owners carry all the liabilities. *See* partnership, sole trader.

See also limited liability company.

unions *See* trade unions.

United Nations (UN) conventions Standards and practices established by the UN and often adopted by individual countries as standards they wish to implement in their own countries.

These conventions are increasingly coming in conflict with domestic government policies.

unlimited liability Personal responsibility by sole traders or those in partnerships for the debts of the businesses they own. Also mutual funds which hold assets as investments may also have unlimited liability, although their asset strength may negate this risk.

Where sole traders or partnerships fail, personal assets will need to be sold to pay creditors. Bankruptcy can result if there are only limited assets to sell.

unrealised gain/loss Pertains to an investment or portfolio where the cost of acquisition is different from the current market price. Until the underlying security is sold any gain or loss is said to be 'unrealised'.

Professional portfolio managers may be required to account for such unrealised gains or losses so as to properly inform investors of their true position.

unsecured creditors People or businesses that are owed money by a business and have not been given any security for the debt. They are usually suppliers who have granted credit for goods or services, family and friends who have loaned money, the tax department for GST or PAYG instalments and employees who are

In the event of administration, receivership or liquidation for a company (or bankruptcy of a sole trader or partnership), unsecured creditors will only be paid after secured creditors.

due wages/salaries or superannuation instalments in their super funds. Certain unsecured creditors (eg. employees, tax departments) do have a priority after secured creditors in a winding up. *See also* secured creditors.

Owners and shareholders are last to be paid, if at all.

unsecured notes Debt securities issued by a company which are unsecured and hence pay a higher than normal rate of interest return. Usually only issued by companies of high reputation and status with a sound record.

Companies may issue such notes as convertible notes which then revert to shares at some future time.

user-friendly Convenient to use, easy to follow, simply explained or tailored to suit people. These expressions are used in business when referring to a work environment. A business is said to be family-friendly when crèche facilities and/or rostered work periods are available.

Often refers to instruction manuals or technical procedures that have been simplified.

utilities Important services provided to the community such as electricity, water, gas and sewerage. A utility may operate as a public listed company or a government enterprise.

AGL, Sydney Water, Natural Gas Australia, Energex and EnviroStar are examples.

V

value-added management Where steps in the production chain add value to the component. The business that can add

The GST is a tax applying to the value-added component of production. Dairy

value to its existing product/service base is also applying value-added management and will enhance its ability to increase sales, customers and potential profits.

companies that diversify milk and butter products and telephone companies which offer other user services are examples of value-added management.

value-added tax (VAT) In the United Kingdom (UK) the VAT is the standard taxation on goods and services. In Australia we have the Goods and Services Tax: *see* GST.

variable costs Expenses that vary with the level of production in a business. Variable costs plus fixed costs makes up total costs. When revenues equal total costs in a business (the break-even point), there is neither a profit nor a loss.

Examples of variable costs are wages, electricity, transport and plant maintenance. A fixed cost would be rent. *See also* fixed costs, break-even point.

variance The difference between planned costs (budgeted) and actual costs. Shown in production reports, monthly profit reports on expenses or in any other report where such variations need highlighting for management action.

Variances must be managed positively since a continuation of adverse variances will impact on business profits.

veil of incorporation A term often used to differentiate between shareholders in a company and the company as a separate legal entity. Means that the assets of the directors of a company can be protected from creditors should the business fail.

venture capital Money invested in a business as commencement capital. Used to either enable research into the viability

Banks have been traditionally reluctant to risk this area of

V

of an idea or product, or as additional equity capital from investors who frequently take a supervisory role over the business. The development of a good business plan is a first step towards gaining venture capital. Also known as *seed capital.*

new ventures. Specialist venture capital companies, however, will take equity in potentially rewarding opportunities.

vertical integration The integration of either a supply (backward) business or a wholesaler (forward) business into an operation to improve costs savings and control for the main business. The investment by BHP in coal mining to supply its steel operations is an example of vertical integration, as is the investment by News Corporation into satellite technology.

Other examples are AGL into gas production and distribution, Coles-Myer into distribution, Leighton into crane hire, etc.

videoconferencing The act of communicating by phone line with a video camera so that each party or group can discuss matters openly using a visual aid. Many businesses now prefer to see and hear when speaking with their suppliers or customers. The reduction in travel time and costs is an outcome of such an activity.

With globalisation and the increasing requirement for transnational corporations to communicate effectively, videoconferencing facilities are being used more often.

virtual office An office that no longer needs to be located within the confines of the business which it serves. Increasingly businesspeople are able to locate at home or in transit through use of laptop computers, mobile phones and Internet cafes.

For example, the use of paralegals drawing on precedent documentation in a home environment and the professionals' personal assistants taking appointments at home or in transit is growing.

vision A simple statement about where a business expects to be in the longer term, for example, in five years. This allows year-by-year planning which does not lose sight of the long-term objectives of the business.

vision statement The commitment in writing for all staff, suppliers and customers as to what the business wants to achieve in the longer term, for example, in five years. Such a statement may include such terms as 'Leading supplier of quality products to a diversified global market, offering maximum opportunities for Australia and staff, with a pre-eminent service to our customer base'.

While the vision statement embodies a more long-term goal, the *mission statement* is more immediate and reachable within 1–2 years. *See also* mission statement.

voidable (unfair) preference Where an action by a business to give a supplier a payment due ahead of another supplier whose account may be older and for no other valid reason. Such preferences may be void in the event of a winding up.

Businesses in trouble have sought to favour certain creditors ahead of others. The directors risk having such payments made void and thus recovered from the paid party.

volatility Refers to extreme or irregular fluctuations of price, volume or of any other measure.

Volatility in a share price would warrant investigation by the ASX and by shareholders.

voluntary administration Where a business appoints an administrator (always a registered and chartered/certified public accountant) to firstly take control of the business to

The business itself takes the initiative. If the administrator is able to trade the business out of

endeavour to trade out of its difficulties, and/or move to wind up the business, taking into account the respective creditor priorities.

its difficulties then the owners may again control the business, but creditors must be informed.

voluntary winding up The action initiated by either the shareholders/directors of a company or by creditors in seeking that a business agree to wind up without compulsion. Such action must be supported by a statutory declaration of solvency from the directors.

75% of shareholders need to approve such action.

W

wage fixing Usually refers to the process undertaken by the Australian Industrial Relations Commission (AIRC) whereby wages and conditions are negotiated with registered bodies representing unions (ACTU), employers, the Australian Chamber of Commerce and Industry, social welfare groups and governments.

The process is undertaken at regular intervals. Government would represent its case in line with its policy parameters. National wage fixing is centralised except where decentralised negotiations occur with enterprise bargaining.

Wireless Application Protocol (WAP) Software included in mobile phones that permits access to the Internet for t-commerce, email and other related activities.

warehousing **(1)** The storing of raw materials, components and finished goods in a planned, well-organised, controlled and easily accessible area for a business. **(2)** The holding of financial securities owned by one party, but ostensibly controlled and appearing to be owned by another, so as to accumulate more securities with minimum public awareness.

The accumulation of certain public listed securities without first making a public offer may be illegal. Similarly, using warehousing with the intention of breaching stock exchange rules is also illegal.

warranties Both specific and implied conditions when products and services are sold which certify that the goods are fit for their purpose, are capable of doing the job, are of merchantable quality and meet the description. This also includes a set period where the goods are guaranteed to perform to contract and where the supplier will remedy any defect.

Businesses would replace or repair products which might be defective. In extreme cases of failure, damages may be awarded in a court action.

warrants Financial contracts similar to options which are structured to give holders certain benefits when they are exercised. For example, a *debt warrant* is exercisable into a debt security, an *equity warrant* offers shares, a *killer warrant* forces redemption of a security, and a *naked warrant* is issued alone. (This list of exotic names is typical of the derivatives market.)

Warrants provide the right to buy a specific amount of the underlying securities and they can be traded if in a listed company.

wastage Usually used in relation to leftover material that potentially could be better used and thus is avoidable. This may occur through manual production

Programmed production processes tend to maximise material use and minimise wastage. The methods, lack of good supervision, non-use of computer machinery and poor staff training. Wastage is an unnecessary cost to a business. Production processes generate waste material, much of which may be reprocessed into some other useful product. Other waste is discarded and may be a pollutant requiring formal disposal.

costs of excessive waste are substantial and new industries are arising from utilising industrial waste products, eg. turning fire ash into building blocks.

wholesaling An intermediary business usually acting for manufacturers by on-selling their products to retailers under agency agreements. Wholesalers are responsible for ensuring retailers are properly stocked, checking that the products are set out in preferred layouts and taking orders for replacement. Wholesalers may obtain commissions for sales volume.

With the rise of the Internet many manufacturers are reviewing the role of intermediaries such as wholesalers, agents and retailers. This process of disintermediation is forcing all businesses to review their marketing distribution systems.

winding up The process carried out under the rules established for sole traders, partnerships and companies in the *Corporations Law* to ultimately sell all the assets of a business for the benefit of lenders, employees, creditors, government and, where possible, investors and owners. Winding up procedures are complex and various avenues may be taken depending on who takes the action. Secured lenders often initiate action by appointing a receiver. *See also* liquidation, voluntary winding up.

Also known as liquidation. There are several ways to wind up an enterprise: members' voluntary administration, creditors' voluntary winding up, compulsory winding up and provisional liquidation.

workstation An area with resources and certain facilities allocated to an employee for carrying out their allotted tasks.

work-in-progress/process That production that is currently under action. It may be piece work, batch production, a process which stops at each day's end or a continual process which may be valued at cost plus the measure of input costs added to it at a particular time.

Inventories comprise raw materials, components, work-in-progress and finished goods. These are usually valued quarterly, six-monthly and at each year-end for reporting purposes.

work-to-rule Where employees and employers are in dispute and employees are only prepared to work in accordance with established award minimums. *See also* go-slow.

An example of work-to-rule may be where the work conditions are too hot and therefore this is a means to obtain airconditioning.

worker participation Involving the workforce in either the management of a business through selection of suitable representatives, or extending the potential of workers to hold shares in a business and thus participate in dividends declared by the business.

Businesses that involve their employees more in management and profit-sharing tend to be more successful and obtain greater employee loyalty.

workers compensation Insurance policy required to be taken by all employers who employ labour. Premiums paid by employers are based on a percentage of employee wages/salaries within an industry type and are paid to nominated insurance companies.

The purpose of this compulsory policy is to enable an employee who is injured in the workplace to be paid while unable to work, plus compensation if justified.

work ethic The attitudes, commitment, behaviour and philosophy to work. The

Some people continually seek knowledge to

work ethic of people can be influenced by a poor environment, inadequate direction or management and personality issues.

advance whilst others are happy to just do the job within requirements.

working capital The money available to a business for day-to-day trading and calculated by deducting current liabilities from current assets. A business that has no working capital would be in crisis and would be classed as insolvent if unable to pay its debts as they fall due.

The current ratio and liquidity (quick asset) ratios are liquidity/solvency ratios seeking to identify forthcoming cash problems in a business.

working capital management Involves the continual management of receivables and inventories by collecting money on time, controlling adequacy of funds and using Just-in-Time policies. Includes also the supervision of financial adequacy, as a cash shortage can see credit curtailed by suppliers. A term loan greater than five years can increase working capital but short-term borrowing will not.

Working capital can also be increased by introducing more equity or by sale and leaseback of existing plant and equipment, motor cars or property.

world best practice (WBP) A policy sometimes accepted by business to adopt, apply and adapt the best methods and practices from around the world in production, marketing, administration, IT, research and development in a business. This is based on the best benchmarks or standards for comparison. It assumes that what is best for one is best for all, but competition, maintaining a sustainable competitive advantage and the costs involved often do not see WBP implemented.

While this concept is highly desirable, it has a cost, which may be prohibitive when applied. Too often the application of WBP has resulted in price increases and reduced sales. There must always be a mutual advantage to the business and the customer.

World Trade Organisation (WTO) An international organisation based in Geneva, Switzerland which aims to facilitate trade between all countries, ideally on a 'level playing field'. For example, Japan endeavoured to restrict rice imports, the USA has sought to restrict steel products, and government subsidies to farmers in some countries are deemed unfair. The overall intention is to bring less developed countries into greater trading of their products and hence to increase their standards of living. *See also* level playing field.

Trade practices that are unfair are monitored and pressure is placed on delinquent countries to abide by the intention of the WTO. Countries that use tariffs, quotas and other trade restrictions must address their commitment to this body. Membership is by invitation or application.

Y

yield The return on an investment related to the current price and expressed as a yield. Applied to dividends as a *dividend yield*, calculated as dividend per share divided by the current market share price. Also applied to earnings as an *earnings yield*, calculated as the earnings per share (EPS) divided by the current market price of the share. The yield to maturity on a commercial bill is calculated when such a bill may be traded and is the rate of interest expressed as a percentage per annum on the amount outlaid.

Examples:

$$\frac{\text{Dividend per share } 20\text{ c}}{\text{Current share price } 400}$$

Dividend yield = 5%

$$\frac{\text{Earnings per share } 15\text{ c}}{\text{Current share price } 162}$$

Earnings yield = 9.26%

Amount outlaid when buying a bill for $100 000 at a yield of 17.25% for 90 days is = $ 95 920.11.

Z

zero defect A term used by a manufacturer meaning that no defect will be permitted in its quality control program. Such surveillance of quality should improve product acceptance and reduce costs and after-sales warranties. Profits should be enhanced.

Quality control programs will assist in this objective. *See also* TQM, quality circles, quality control.

zoning Land-use categorisation as applied by local councils. For example, residential zoning may be Category A, commercial may be Category B, light industrial may be Category C zoning, etc.